IMAGES OF WAR

PARTISAN WARFARE
ON THE
EASTERN FRONT
1941–1944

S. E. Pisarevich, a member of the 'Partisan Brigade Buddeny'. This formation fought in the Pinsk region. A unit in this area 'destroyed four railway bridges, three water pump houses ... and burned down a railway sleeper production plant', as described in an Army Group Centre report.

IMAGES OF WAR

PARTISAN WARFARE ON THE EASTERN FRONT 1941–1944

RARE PHOTOGRAPHS FROM WARTIME ARCHIVES

Nik Cornish

Pen & Sword
MILITARY

First published in Great Britain in 2013 by
PEN & SWORD MILITARY
an imprint of
Pen & Sword Books Ltd,
47 Church Street,
Barnsley,
South Yorkshire
S70 2AS

ISBN 978 184884 376 9

A CIP record for this book is available from the British Library.

Typeset by CHIC GRAPHICS

Printed and bound by CPI Group (UK) Ltd, Croydon, CR0 4YY

Pen & Sword Books Ltd incorporates the Imprints of
Pen & Sword Aviation, Pen & Sword Family History, Pen & Sword Maritime, Pen & Sword Military, Pen & Sword Discovery, Wharncliffe Local History, Wharncliffe True Crime, Wharncliffe Transport, Pen & Sword Select, Pen & Sword Military Classics, Leo Cooper, The Praetorian Press, Remember When, Seaforth Publishing and Frontline Publishing.

For a complete list of Pen & Sword titles please contact
Pen & Sword Books Limited
47 Church Street, Barnsley, South Yorkshire, S70 2AS, England
E-mail: enquiries@pen-and-sword.co.uk
Website: www.pen-and-sword.co.uk

Contents

Acknowledgements

It would have been impossible to write this book without the assistance of Dmitry Belanovsky who introduced me to the two partisan veterans, Dr Albert Tsessarsky and Boris Chorny, my interviews with whom provide the human interest quoted later. It is to them and to the countless thousands of partisans who fought, suffered and died in this greatest of all People's Wars that this book is dedicated with my humble thanks for their untold sacrifices. Further thanks are due to Andrei Simonov and Norbert Hofer.

This book is dedicated to my Mum Dorothy, my partner Angie and to my children Charlotte, Alex and James.

Photographic Sources

Images are taken from the following sources:

Courtesy of the Central Museum of the Armed Forces, Moscow via www.stavka.org.uk: pp. 16, 21B, 23T, 27T, 29T, 40, 41T, 43B, 50T, 51T, 52B, 53B, 54B, 57B, 58B, 69T, 70, 77, 79, 80B, 81T, 82B, 91, 93T, 97B, 99B, 100T, 108B, 109B, 110T, 111, 113B, 114, 119T, 120T, 122B, 124, 125B, 126, 127T, 128B, 134T, 135T, 136, 138T, 139B, 140T, 141, 143, 144.

From the fonds of the RGAKFD, Krasnogorsk via www.stavka.org.uk: pp. 2, 13B, 23B, 25, 26, 28T, 34, 35, 36T, 39, 44T, 51B, 56T, 57T, 64T, 65B, 66B, 67T, 69B, 78T, 80T, 82T, 83, 84, 85T, 92, 94, 97T, 98, 99T, 100B, 107, 108T, 109T, 112T, 122T, 127B, 133, 135B, 142.

From Nik Cornish at www.stavka.org.uk: pp. 13T, 14, 15, 21T, 22, 24, 27B, 28B, 29B, 30, 36B, 37, 38, 41B, 42, 43T, 44B, 49, 50B, 52T, 53T, 54T, 55, 56B, 58T, 63, 64B, 65T, 66T, 67B, 68, 71, 72, 78B, 85N, 86, 93B, 95, 96, 105, 106, 110B, 112B, 113T, 119B, 120B, 121, 123, 125T, 128T, 134B, 137, 138B, 139T, 140B.

From the Andrei Simonov Collection: p. 81B.

Preface

The purpose of this book is straightforward: it aims to provide the reader with a broad-brush picture of the war behind the lines on the Eastern Front – the personalities, the campaigns, its horrors and its effects.

In 2003 I was privileged to be able to meet and interview two former partisans, Boris Chorny and Dr Albert Tsessarsky, living in retirement in Moscow. As with many veterans, they were happy to talk about their experiences, whilst glossing over any incidents that cast a shadow across the stories of partisan heroism which remains the official line in Russia today. I have a huge respect for such men, their bravery, their achievements and their loyalty to their comrades and their beliefs. I have used the information they provided me with throughout this book as it gives a human touch to what could otherwise be described as a 'laundry list' of units and actions.

Remarkably for such a campaign, official photographers accompanied several of the partisan units and recorded what they saw for posterity. The images in this book draw on archives held in the former Soviet Union under the headings of: the partisan groups and the occupied territories.

Axis images have been taken from my private collection, built up over several years. Official images are included but the vast majority are from individuals who recorded events on unofficially carried cameras.

Any study of the partisan war that raged behind the Axis lines in the USSR between 1941 and 1944 immediately raises contentious issues such as did the USSR include the Baltic republics of Lithuania, Latvia and Estonia occupied by the Red Army in 1940? What of the Romanian territory between the rivers Bug and Dniester annexed by the Soviet Union in 1940 or western Ukraine taken from Poland in 1939?

In a book of this length and nature it is necessary to recognise and acknowledge these questions and their importance, but it is impossible to research and discuss them with the detail they merit.

I do not claim to shed any new light on what, for many citizens of the former USSR, is still a highly controversial issue. However, I hope that there are some amongst the readers of this book who will take a deeper interest in this topic. If nothing else, I will be pleased if readers gain a somewhat clearer picture of the tangled web that was the partisan war in the USSR from 1941–1944.

Introduction

Over the past two decades the massive contribution of the Soviet Union's armed forces to the defeat of Hitler's Germany and its allies during the Second World War has been increasingly understood and recognised as layers of political propaganda have been peeled away and reality has replaced official, Communist Party, 'truths'. Indeed, the casualties, the suffering and genocide endured by citizens of the Soviet Union during the Second World War are still a matter of close study in the former USSR.

Partisan and guerrilla warfare can be loosely defined and differentiated in the following manner. Partisan troops are those members or affiliated members of the armed forces that are operating behind enemy lines, whereas guerrillas are generally civilians fighting against an occupying force. However, both terms are often used indiscriminately. In addition, the situation is not helped by the Axis use of the umbrella term partisans only to replace it with bandits to highlight the illegal and outlaw nature of the fighters.

In fact, partisans/guerrillas have a long and honourable lineage in Russian and Soviet military history stretching back to the Napoleonic Wars, when partisan units of Cossack and other mounted troops waged war on the Grand Army's supply lines and rear before and during the retreat from Moscow. During the First World War partisan operations were undertaken by Cossacks and regular cavalry, groups of which infiltrated behind German and Austrian lines to carry out disruptive missions such as blowing up railway lines, intelligence gathering and kidnapping. Specialist units were established in the Cossack formations by order of the Grand Duke Boris Vladimirovitch, the *Ataman* of Cossack forces at the front during 1915, but reports on their achievements were such that the majority were disbanded. Nevertheless, some units, such as Shkuro's Wolves, acquitted themselves well. Following the revolution of March 1917, Russia's armed forces began to go into gradual decline and as that fateful year drew to a close the Bolshevik coup of November led to open civil war that spread across the empire now turned republic. Over the next four years partisan and guerrilla formations of all shapes, sizes and levels of effectiveness flashed across the vastness of Russia from the mountains of the Caucasus, across the steppes of Ukraine, the tundra and forests of Siberia to the coastlines of the Pacific Ocean. As the Soviet government emerged from the civil war victorious and extended its somewhat tenuous grip across the provinces, names such as that of Chapayev became known to the public of the USSR as one of the partisan leaders who had contributed to the destruction of 'interventionists and counter revolutionaries'. Indeed, the lauding of partisan leaders and groups formed almost a staple of Soviet popular culture into the mid-1930s. Furthermore, the value of partisan warfare was seriously studied by the higher echelons of the Soviet military.

In parallel, Soviet military theory during the 1920s and into the 1930s included the use of partisan formations to disrupt invaders' lines of supply, communications and reinforcement.

Plans were laid for the establishment of secret bases along anticipated invasion routes to supply partisan groups who would train in the use of 'captured weapons and equipment'. Local forces would be supported by specialists, such as radio operators and demolition experts, who would be parachuted in. Some work and training was undertaken by the Ukrainian Military District in the years leading up to 1936. However, Stalin, increasingly suspicious of the armed forces, was, like Hitler, a military theorist and a firm believer in the offensive as the ultimate strategy. Furthermore, any thoughts that a war would be fought on Soviet territory were anathema to him. Equally unappealing was the prospect of encouraging and arming elements of the populace in the very areas where famine, disease and starvation stalked the land in the wake of his disastrous agricultural policy of forced collectivisation. Training such victims in the ways of partisan and guerilla warfare was not to be encouraged. Consequently, as the infamous purges of the armed forces decimated the officer corps, thoughts of any war waged on Soviet land was replaced by offensive operations beyond the frontiers and the partisan bases already built were allowed to revert to their natural condition whilst the plans mouldered on shelves in the archives. Another major aspect of partisan warfare that Stalin wished actively to eliminate was the very set of characteristics that made for effective leadership in partisan groups: the ability to think and plan independently beyond the control of Moscow; the capacity to adapt to local circumstances as required; and the charisma to hold together such a group in times of danger and low morale. Lumped together, these characteristics were known disparagingly as *Partisanshchina* – a trait not to be encouraged in a totalitarian regime.

It was the shock of the Axis invasion that would regenerate the need for partisan warfare on a scale unimaginable only a few years before as the people, not only the armed forces, would be called upon to fight a ruthless invader.

An interesting group, which the original caption implies was a part of a partisan unit formed in 1915 for operations behind German lines. Although most of their clothing is Russian, the figure to the left is wearing what appears to be a German-style tunic.

The legendary First World War and Russian Civil War partisan cavalry unit known as 'Shkuro's Wolves', pictured in 1919 during a lull in anti-Bolshevik operations. Recruited from Kuban Cossacks, the Wolves were named after their wolf-skin standard and *papakhas* (hat).

Locally recruited Basmachi guerrillas pose with their Soviet commissar and advisor. During the 1920s elements of the native populations of the Soviet Union's central Asian provinces waged an unsuccessful war against their Russian masters.

Air power was recognised by the Soviets as one of the most important weapons in the battle against guerrillas and partisans. Pilot P. Leykin, who flew his machine against anti-Soviet forces in the Caucasus during 1920, is seen here.

The German military had experience of partisan/guerrilla warfare from its days as the colonial power in German East Africa (present-day Tanzania) when local uprisings were put down with ruthless brutality. These bandsmen are members of the German colonial forces. Indeed, a nephew of the German commander in this region when they suffered their greatest defeat rose to become head of Germany's anti-bandit (partisan) warfare on the Eastern Front.

During 1918 the Central Powers occupied vast swathes of Ukraine and southern Russia. Apart from taking Russia out of the war, the main purpose of the occupation was to provide food for the populations of Austria-Hungary and Germany by requisitioning from the farmers of these areas. When the quota was not forthcoming reprisals led to armed confrontations with ad hoc guerrilla groups, many members of which were ex-soldiers. One such is shown here following his execution by the Austro-Hungarian authorities.

Chapter One

'A Cry of Despair'
Hitler's Comment on Stalin's Broadcast

On 22 June 1941 Hitler launched Operation Barbarossa – the invasion of the USSR – but the frontiers his troops crossed that Sunday morning were not those of the late 1930s. Between 1939 and 1941 the borders of the Soviet Union had moved dramatically westwards, absorbing the Baltic States, Galicia, a large chunk of Poland, and the Romanian provinces of Bessarabia and North Bukovina. Although these nations and regions had formed part of the tsarist empire and included ethnic Russian minorities, they were largely non-Russian in composition. Indeed, an influx of Russian administrators and a policy of Russification combined with Communist practices, such as collectivisation, had done much to alienate the population of these new acquisitions, as did the ruthless purges of 'undesirable elements'. Tens of thousands were executed, imprisoned and deported, deportations of Poles and Ukrainians continuing until Friday 20 June 1941, presumably to be resumed after the weekend. The NKVD (the acronym for the People's Commissariat for Internal Affairs), headed by L. P. Beria, was as effective as Himmler's SS at removing those deemed unreliable or a threat to the regime. Thus it was that the population in many border regions greeted the invaders with great enthusiasm anticipating a dramatic improvement in their lives.

But, as thousands of locals cheered and even took pot shots at retreating Soviet troops during the last week of June and into July, Moscow was recovering from its initial horror at the events on its western borders. On 3 July Stalin broadcast to the people of the USSR. Candidly admitting German successes in Lithuania, western Belarus, Latvia and western Ukraine, he continued calling for a scorched earth policy in the face of the enemy advance but behind enemy lines:

> In areas occupied by the enemy guerrilla units, mounted and on foot must be formed, diversionist groups must be organised to combat enemy troops, to foment guerrilla warfare everywhere, to blow up bridges and roads, damage

telephone and telegraph lines, set fire to forests, stores, transports. In the occupied regions conditions must be made unbearable for the enemy and all his accomplices. They must be hounded and annihilated at every step and all their measures frustrated ... All forces of the people for the demolition of the enemy.

This speech also cast Hitler and his Fascist followers as the aggressors and the 'Russians, Ukrainians, Belorussians, Lithuanians, Latvians, Moldavians, Georgians, Estonians ... and the other free people of the Soviet Union' as the victims.

Having given his blessing to the formation of partisan units, the state apparatus swung into action. On a local level the Communist Party began to organise the nuclei of partisan groups. In Moscow the military and civilian government leadership formed the State Defence Committee (GKO) and military authority was incorporated into the Stavka (Supreme Command), both headed by Stalin himself.

Fifteen days after Stalin's broadcast the Central Committee of the Communist Party issued detailed instructions to regional Party organisations. Local Party leaders were ordered to organise resistance themselves, 'to destroy the hoarders and their collaborators ... to put an end to such unbearable conditions [whereby] leaders of the Party leave their posts and retreat deep into the rear . . . thus becoming deserters and pitiful cowards'. Partisan leaders were encouraged to recruit members from 'particularly reliable, leading Party, Soviet, and Komsomol (the Communist youth organisation) and also non-Party members devoted to the Soviet regime'. Personnel were to have knowledge of the local population, the area and the terrain. A network of saboteurs and specialists was to support the fighters, as would propagandists. Local formations were to be divided into companies, platoons and sections with responsibility for a specified area of operations. Membership was to be voluntary and, at least in the early days, the leadership was to be elected. Bases were to be well concealed and stores laid in. Although this directive did not create more than a rough template for partisan organisation, it did specify that such groups should arm themselves, train and take guidance from the headquarters' staff made up of 'members of the executive committees of the regional, district and village Soviets'. There was no mention of co-ordination with the Red Army, this was purely a Party structure.

Appropriately, considering its role as the guardian of the USSR's internal security, the NKVD was also setting up its own partisan fiefdom. On 5 July the Administration for Special Tasks was activated. Amongst its portfolio of duties was the establishment of partisan formations. The unit title for its organisation was the Separate Motorised Rifle Brigade of Special Purpose. Amongst its 20,000 men and women, including 2,000 foreigners – Germans, Austrians, Spaniards, Poles, Czechs and Americans to name but a few, were hundreds of sportsmen and women, members of rifle clubs and those deemed fit enough for the rigours of life behind enemy lines.

Whilst this formation underwent training near Moscow, the NKVD organised from its provincial staff so-called Destruction Battalions, which were responsible for security behind the Red Army's lines. They were to guard against air-dropped saboteurs and agent provocateurs but, should the Red Army fall back, they would carry out the destruction of any useful infrastructure such as power stations or railway depots. They were to allow themselves to be bypassed by the enemy and then to re-emerge to carry out acts of sabotage and wage a war of terror against local collaborators. They would wear civilian clothing and live off the land. Again, there was no direct mention of co-ordinating their activities with the Red Army which implied a mutual distrust likely based on the NKVD's activities during the purges of recent memory and the perception of the military's failure to defend Mother Russia during the early days of Barbarossa.

The third body to become involved in the partisan war was the Red Army itself. The sheer speed of the Axis advance had taken the Soviets completely by surprise as the panzers overran defensive positions so rapidly that formations simply dissolved. As Moscow sought desperately for solutions it dispatched orders that were out of date or were never received. Frequently, these orders were obeyed for fear of reprisals leading to the loss of scores of thousands of troops and mountains of equipment. In a series of vast pincer movements the Axis surrounded divisions, corps and armies by the dozen. Hundreds of thousands of bewildered POWs were marched westwards, often under minimal guard. However, for those Red Army men and officers isolated but still motivated and able to fight there were the alternatives of making their way back to their own lines or forming partisan groups. Unfortunately, many of those who escaped captivity or were not captured returned to their side of the line unaware of Order 270, dated 16 August 1941. In this Stalin declared that every soldier was obliged to 'fight to the last (and) forbidden to surrender', otherwise he would be considered a deserter and either shot or arrested for such an offence. The core of those groups who could not get back to their lines and chose to fight as partisans were often officers or NCOs and they became known as *Okruzhentsy* (those who escaped the encirclement). Political officers were often ordered to remain behind to continue the fight as their formations disintegrated.

As early as 25 June Army Group Centre (AGC), heading eastwards through Belorussia, noted 'stragglers and guerrillas' were attacking supply convoys, field hospitals and security troops. Army Group South (AGS) advancing towards Kiev seemed uniquely untroubled by such activities.

Army Group North (AGN), on the other hand, was plagued by groups of Red

Army stragglers that attacked any vulnerable target. Such army partisan groups were more cohesive, trained, recently blooded and disciplined. But as well as these ad hoc bands the Red Army issued its own organisational instructions regarding partisan formations and the tasks they should undertake. Interestingly, there is no particular reference to Party memberships as a prerequisite for recruitment:

> Partisan detachments must be well-armed and sufficiently strong for active operations in the enemy rear. The total strength of such a unit may amount to 75–150 men organised into two or three companies with the companies divided into two or three platoons. The basic operating section of the combat units will be the company and the platoon. Their basic duties – carried out as a rule at night or from ambush – are attacks on columns and concentrations of motorised infantry, on supply dumps and ammunition transports, on airfields and railway transports.

Again, the units were to be based on local administrative areas, 'each of which should contain at least one partisan combat unit'. Higher authority, 'above the level of the individual unit, exists only for the purpose of controlling their operations and organising new groups'. In addition,

> Party, Soviet offices and the representatives of the NKVD are fully responsible for the organisation of the Destruction Battalions and their conversion into partisan units. It is categorically forbidden to dissolve the Destruction Battalions; if they split up or retreat into our [Red Army] rear areas, the head of the above named offices will be brought to account before the War Tribunal.

This threat was followed by detailed instructions on how to carry out operations of all types against the enemy, including the damaging of railway track by loosening 'the rails with the help of a wrench, which is available in every signalman's hut'.

The directive also reminded the partisans that 'the partisan movement splinters, tires out and weakens the forces of the enemy and brings about advantageous conditions for the Red Army's counter attack'. The document quoted from Stalin's 3 July speech and concluded, 'undermine all his [the Axis] measures, do not wait for the assignment of tasks from above . . . operate independently'.

German, Soviet and Polish officers meet to discuss terms following the division of Poland between the Third Reich and the USSR. The reincorporation of western Ukraine into the Soviet Union led to a wave of purges that devastated the intelligentsia and generated an upsurge of anti-Soviet feeling. When the partisan war began in earnest mistrust between Soviet and Polish partisan groups was intense.

However, myths regarding the power of the Red Army were abruptly called into question as a result of their lacklustre campaign against the Finns during the winter of 1939–1940. Although ultimately victorious, the Soviets suffered high losses in men and materiel due to their weak tactical leadership and poor winter equipment.

German troops inspect a captured French vehicle in June 1940. The speed and success of the German campaigns in Western Europe gave rise to a sense of German invincibility amongst some elements of the Soviet military and civilian hierarchy.

Men of a German infantry regiment on the border of the USSR listen to a briefing hours before the opening of Operation Barbarossa. Much of their political indoctrination consisted of lectures on the nature of the *untermensch* (sub-humans) they would be fighting.

Blissfully unaware of the Axis preparations just hundreds of metres away over the border, Soviet riflemen wash themselves during the warm weather of late June 1941. Within days many would be POWs, casualties or hiding in the swamps and forests.

On the streets of Leningrad Soviet citizens listen to the news, broadcast through loudspeakers, that the USSR has been invaded. It was the voice of Molotov, Stalin's deputy and Commissar for Foreign Affairs, that announced the Fascist aggression. Ironically, this broadcast was heard in cities close to the fighting following on from keep-fit programmes. In the wake of this broadcast hundreds of thousands of Russians volunteered to fight.

Some of the hundreds of thousands of Red Army men captured during the summer and autumn of 1941. Escorted by tiny numbers of Axis personnel, many POWs slipped away into hiding and formed the nuclei of partisan bands. The remainder stayed in captivity and suffered untold hardships. AGC issued a proclamation stating that, 'All Russian soldiers found west of the Berezina River after 15 August would be considered as partisans and treated as such.'

The welcome received by Axis forces in western Ukraine was remarkable. This German encampment outside a village shows a decorative arch prepared by the locals. It reads 'Heil Hitler' and shows a swastika next to the Ukrainian symbol the trident of Vladimir.

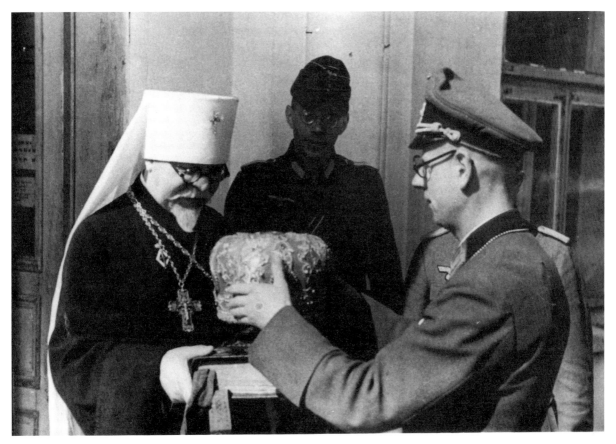

A senior priest receives regalia from a German Army chaplain. The reinstatement of the churches both in western Ukraine and other areas of the occupied territories gained the Axis much in the way of support during the early months of Operation Barbarossa.

In the wake of the panzers came the men of the four Einsatzgruppen (Action Groups) who were to carry out Hitler's ethnic-cleansing policies. Here a group of Jews marked with the Star of David sort captured Red Army impedimenta. Many of the Soviet bureaucrats in the newly acquired western lands were Russian-Jewish giving credence to Hitler's racial/political policies.

A senior German officer receives a delegation of Galician civilians in Lvov. Following the Soviet withdrawal nationalists called for independence. This request was rejected by the German authorities. Ukrainian nationalist groups continued to press for a greater degree of local autonomy.

As Russian railways operated on a broader gauge track is was essential for the Axis engineer units to replace them with the narrower European version. Such work was undertaken by local civilians who laboured around the clock regardless of accidents. The lack of metalled roads meant that the railways were the major transport system utilised by the Axis in the USSR.

From all over the USSR recruits were rushed to the west to replace the staggering losses during the early weeks of campaigning. Hurled pell-mell into the struggle, they often ended up cut off, isolated and disoriented behind enemy lines.

Despite the war raging around them, the farmers still had to gather the summer's harvest. Soon, however, the demands of the Axis occupation authorities for supplies for the army and the home markets would begin to reduce any surplus produce to a minimum. Starvation, like that of the 1930s, would return under a different regime.

Summary executions of partisans, Jews, Communists and those perceived to be unreliable were soon a common event in the occupied territories.

Refugees followed and preceded the Red Army's retreat. For those whose work did not entitle them to evacuation walking eastwards was the only alternative. The human cost paid by the USSR as a result of these migrations has yet to be fully evaluated.

But in the forests and marshes groups of partisans were mobilising. This party of mounted men appears to be clad in a mix of civilian and military dress and well armed. The setting gives some idea of the densely wooded areas in the western regions of the USSR.

A German officer poses for a private photograph with an elderly Ukrainian couple. Images such as this were often used by the Axis authorities to reinforce the carefully cultivated impression of the primitive, barbaric, uncivilised nature of the sub-humans they were dealing with.

A German reconnaissance unit wends its way across rolling, featureless steppes of the Ukraine. Such terrain made the concealment of partisan formations well-nigh impossible and limited their movements to the hours of darkness.

Striking back! This German vehicle has been struck by a mine laid by partisans. However, the reprisals meted out to those living nearby are yet to be undertaken.

Chapter Two

'The War in Russia Cannot be Fought in a Knightly Fashion' – Hitler, March 1941

If confusion, bureaucratic muddle and mistrust seemed to reign in Moscow as to how to wage a partisan war, it was equally so, if not greater, in the ministerial halls of Berlin when the questions of security and administration arose. The occupied territories of the western USSR were subject to such a diverse range of aims, policies, jurisdictions, empire building, racial and ideological superiority complexes, inter-agency rivalries, personality clashes, personal agendas and plain stupidity as has been rarely, if ever, equalled in the history of imperialist expansion. Above this seething cauldron squatted the architect of the Third Reich – Adolph Hitler. A master of declaiming a thought that his minions would then translate into orders as suited their requirements, Hitler had ordained that the war against the USSR was a war against an inferior species – the Slav. Rabidly anti-Communist Hitler viewed the USSR as the epitome of everything he loathed politically and racially, a Jew-inspired (Karl Marx), Jew-infested (Trotsky et al.) system that was a greater threat to his world-conquering ambitions than the decadent empires of France and Great Britain. The war in the east was to be one of extermination, a crusade against Bolshevism. His theories were summed up in the so-called Commissar Order of March 1941 and other instructions that collectively became known as the Barbarossa Directives: Soviet officials, Jews and Red Army political officers were to be rounded up and executed. These orders applied to the Waffen (combat) SS, the Wehrmacht (the German armed forces) and the German police units assigned to the Eastern Front. Effectively, all ranks were granted a licence to kill, whatever others in the services thought of them, as 'any German soldier who breaks international law will be pardoned'.

In simplistic terms Operation Barbarossa aimed to destroy the Red Army, take Leningrad, Moscow, Kiev, Kharkov and then to occupy the USSR roughly along the line of the Ural Mountains from Archangel to Astrakhan. Beyond that the rump of the Soviet system was expected to wither away. But west of the Urals would be a land filling up with Aryan settlers farming and working all across the Lebensraum (living space) dreamt of by Hitler. Military colonies would be established to supervise the Slav population, who would work in conditions akin to slavery for the benefit of the Third Reich. Oil from the Caucasus, coal from the Donbass and wheat from Ukraine would all provide for an ever-expanding Nazi empire.

As the Axis armies advanced towards their goals the occupied territories expanded rapidly. In the combat zone the German Army was responsible for rear-area security. Each of the army groups, AGN, AGC and AGS, had a number of security divisions attached to it specifically to undertake this task. The army's nine security divisions were such in name only. They consisted of two regiments, each of three or four battalions, one regiment was 'combat' ready, the other more fitted for sedentary work such as installation or railway guard duties. AGS was better provided for as it could call on five Hungarian brigades grouped together as VIII Army Corps based in Kiev under the title of the Hungarian Occupation Command (HOC). However, they were not popular with the Ukrainians. A German report noted, 'People say that the Hungarians are worse than the Bolsheviks ... confiscate all food, show sympathy to Poles and Jews'. In common with German security troops, the Hungarians were poorly equipped but such arms as they possessed were adequate for guarding railway lines and bridges during the summer and autumn of 1941. Slovakian and Romanian security formations, though not as numerous as the Hungarians, were also on hand, although the Romanians were mainly deployed in Transnistria and Odessa.

As the fighting zone moved eastwards security then became the job of other agencies. The largest of these was the SS which had a Higher SS and Police Leader (HSSPF) behind every army group. Each commanded a police regiment of three battalions. As well as these troops, three Waffen SS brigades, two infantry and one cavalry were available to supplement the police. Alongside these was a smaller group, four battalions, of colonial police commanded by SS Oberst Gruppenfuhrer Karl Daluege. All were answerable to Himmler as Reichsfuhrer SS. A born intriguer and empire builder, Himmler viewed the eastern campaign as an ideal opportunity to expand his power and influence beyond control of the police and the four Waffen SS combat divisions.

However, on 17 July 1941 Hitler appointed Alfred Rosenberg, a Baltic German émigré and ardent Nazi, as Reich Minister for the Occupied Eastern Territories. His remit was simple, to oversee the administration of four projected Reich Commissariats: Ostland (the Baltic States and much of Belorussia), Ukraine (including Crimea), Muscovy and the Caucasus. The latter two were stillborn. The Bukovina and Bessarabia were returned to Romania as Transnistria. The internal security of these territories was the responsibility of the SS, but Wehrmacht forces operating there remained under army or Luftwaffe control. To further complicate matters, in the combat zone and army group rear areas the SS came under Wehrmacht control.

Hitler did not wish his racial or economic policies to be widely known in the occupied territories, but wanted his bureaucrats to appear to 'occupy, administer and secure a certain area . . . in the interest of the inhabitants . . . We do not wish to make people into enemies prematurely.' Despite this, Hitler announced that Stalin's call for partisan warfare, 'has some advantages for us; it allows us to eradicate everyone who opposes us'. Those easterners who did not oppose the new regime were given the opportunity to join the Schutzmannschaft (shortened to Schuma) police units that Himmler brought into being under the auspices of the colonial police command on 25 July 1941. Within months thousands of Balts, Belorussians and Ukrainians had enlisted in these units and joined their new masters in executing Jews, partisans and Communists.

All the security elements deployed by the Axis had, by the end of 1941, been involved in varying degrees of action with partisan forces. But the partisans possessed one ally that was firmly on their side – the terrain.

The swamps and forests of the western Soviet Union were, and in some cases still are, primeval fastnesses. From the border along the Bug River to Vyazma, some 200km west of Moscow, the landscape was dominated by forests that formed a dense arc starting at Brest Litovsk running through Minsk, Orsha, Smolensk to Vyazma and then south-west to Bryansk and Gomel. Lying between Brest Litovsk and Gomel are the Pripet Marshes, some 400km east to west by roughly 200km north to south; 80,000sq km of soaking morass, almost trackless and varying in depth from 1m to more than 10m. Flowing west to east out of the marshes are the many branched headwaters of the Pripet River, which joins the Dnieper River in swamp lands approximately 100km north of Kiev. North of Minsk the city of Polotsk stood at the base of yet more thick forest that arced north-eastwards through Velikie Luki and along the Valdai Hills south-east of Leningrad. Just west of the Valdai range the Lovat River flowed north into Lake Ilmen, again its banks were low and marshy. From Lake Ilmen the Volkhov River runs down to Lake Ladoga.

South of the forests and swamps of Belorussia and Russia lay the steppes of Ukraine, a rolling relatively woodland free area passing Kiev, Kharkov, Rostov on Don and thence to Stalingrad on the Volga River: kilometre after kilometre of featureless, lightly cultivated or grazed land. South again to the temperate Crimea, here the partisans found sanctuary in the coastal hills and caves of the Yaila range.

To the north the Baltic States presented a mix of rolling steppe and thick, often marshy, forest with little high ground.

The main population centres were Minsk, Kiev, Riga and Kharkov but over 80 per cent of the people were peasant farmers eking out a living in the hope that the new Axis administrators would do away with the collective farms and introduce some economic freedoms. In the thousands of villages and hamlets scattered between the Baltic and Black seas life went on in a fashion that would not have surprised ancestors five centuries previously.

It was into this unfamiliar landscape that the Axis was plunged, quickly discovering that metalled roads outside of the major towns were rare and that the railways were often only single-tracked and poorly maintained. Finding fresh water soon proved to be a massive problem as the local supplies were often too powerful for the more delicate digestive systems of Western Europeans. Water-borne diseases ran through the ranks like a plague as dehydrated men drank anything resembling

Throughout the summer of 1941 the forces of the Axis were greeted as liberators as they advanced into the western Soviet Union. In the Baltic States AGN was particularly welcomed, as seen here. Racially acceptable to the Nazis, the Balts would not experience the full horror of the new regime.

Outside the former Soviet administration building a German officer receives the traditional welcoming gift of salt and bread from a local notable. To the right a German propaganda unit films the event for the German newsreel. However, regime change did not bring any immediate benefits to the people.

water with scant thought for the consequences. The SS, to name one organisation, had not brought sufficient distillation equipment. Indeed, it proved necessary to airlift mineral water and provide special trains to provide clean drinking water to some areas. When the rain did fall it turned the roads to glue-like mud, then the frost was succeeded by the snow that presaged the first winter on the Eastern Front. It was to prove a crucial season for the Axis, but it was even more trying for the partisans all across the bleak landscape of what was now called the Temporarily Occupied Territories, or Little Land. All types of stores were running low. Assistance from the 'Great Land', unoccupied Russia, was sporadic and often non-existent, so for many partisan bands during the first winter of their war it was a matter of survival not combat – that could wait for better times.

Walking in the road as a German soldier passes on the pavement and wearing the Star of David (on the backs of their coats), two Jews in the Reich Commissariat of Ostland are clearly aware of their new status. Anti-Semitism was widespread amongst the population of the newly occupied areas which led to support for and participation in Nazi pogroms.

Men of the SS Cavalry Brigade ride through a village in the rear of AGC. The 1st Regiment was commanded by Hermann Fegelein (who married Eva Braun's sister). The brigade was notorious for its ruthless behaviour, claiming some 17,000 victims, both Jewish and partisan, during July and August 1941.

German police battalions were drafted in as part of the security provision in the occupied territories. However, when called on to plug the gaps in the front line, such formations suffered heavy casualties due to their lack of equipment and training. As they were given a low priority for supplies they often lacked mobility.

Admiral Horthy, the Regent of Hungary, seen here to the left of Hitler, provided security troops for duties in Ukraine. They were less ideologically racist, and, in the words of a former Russian partisan who fought against them, 'At first they were tough, tougher than the Germans but towards the end they surrendered more quickly.'

The Italian contribution to the Eastern Front was numerically impressive, with over 200,000 men assigned to AGS. Their approach to rear-area security appears to have been less ruthless than that of their partners, nor did they contribute significant numbers to such tasks.

Romania's forces engaged in security work were, initially, small and confined to Transnistria. However, regular troops became heavily involved in anti-partisan sweeps in Crimea in 1942–1944. In this theatre the Romanian mountain units proved particularly adept.

Reichsfuhrer Heinrich Himmler (profile, facing left) visited the Eastern Front during the summer of 1941 to gauge the progress of the Einsatzgruppen as they eliminated Jews, Communists and other 'undesirables'. Impressed with the statistics reported, he almost collapsed when watching a mass execution. At that point he ordered that women and children were to be gassed in specially made vans instead of shot.

Witnessing such an event as this mass execution caused Himmler such upset, forcing him to consider the psychological effects of such 'work' on his men. Although these 'aktions' were usually carried out without local witnesses, news spread and led to growing disaffection with the new masters and increasing sympathy for the partisans.

In the absence of secret supply dumps embryonic partisan groups scavenged the battlefields for weapons. This group appears to have been particularly successful, counting mortars, rifles and two machine guns amongst their trophies. Learning how to maintain such arsenals as they possessed proved to be a steep learning curve and involved a large degree of improvisation for men with a minimum of military/technical experience.

The disruption of communications was an easy task to accomplish as it required no more than an axe, as seen here. When repair crews were sent out they often fell victim to snipers. However, with winter drawing in, food and shelter were rapidly becoming a priority.

It was not just arms and equipment that the partisans sought, but also boots and clothing, as the corpses of this German armoured vehicle crew demonstrates. Mines found on the battlefield were frequently dug up and re-sited by Red Army partisans well-practised in their use.

During the summer of 1941 various nationalities of Soviet POWs, including large numbers of Ukrainians, were released from POW camps to return home as long as they worked usefully for the Reich (to paraphrase Hitler). Undoubtedly, large numbers of these lucky men quietly went over to the partisans, although not the group seen here.

Rounding up Red Army stragglers continued well after the fighting had moved east. These men would have then been kept in squalid, unsanitary, wired holding pens, lacking food and other essentials. Sympathy for their plight grew amongst civilians, even in non-Russian areas. Again, such treatment of human beings worked to erode belief in Hitler's future plans. In ethnic Russian territory such overt cruelty acted as a powerful recruitment tool for the partisans.

A very well turned out section of Latvian Schuma with German police officers. Such units were deployed to Belarus and Ukraine as and when required, particularly if similar local troops were of doubtful loyalty.

Happily posing for the camera, two men of a security division attached to the rear of AGC take time out from guarding a railway bridge. Such peaceful moments were to become less frequent as the partisans increased their activities.

As the partisans became a greater problem the Nazi administration resorted to terror as a means of deterrent. As seen here, captured partisans were paraded through the streets of the nearest town on the way to their execution. The sign reads, 'We are partisans we shot at German soldiers'.

Under the watchful eyes of her neighbours, a Russian lady dances with a middle-aged member of a German security unit. Such 'hearts and minds' exercises were increasingly at odds with the realities of life in the occupied territories.

The shape of things to come. In December 1941 all education provision beyond the age of 10 was closed down in all the occupied territories other than the Baltic States. In the words of one high-ranking Nazi, it was sufficient that Russian children be able to read road warnings to avoid disrupting military traffic. Here desks and chairs await the bonfire.

Chapter Three

Winter's Agony, 1941-1942

Although the Soviet response to the Axis invasion may appear to have been muddled, slow and ad hoc, without doubt it took the enemy by surprise by its scale and sheer tenacity. By October 1941 the three security divisions of AGC, along with the SS Cavalry Brigade and the police battalions of the HSSPF, were supposed to secure and impose law and order in an area of 320,000sq km. The rear of AGS was a little better served due to the Allied security troops it was able to draw upon. However, AGN, standing almost at the gates of Leningrad, on Russian soil proper was faced with a significant problem. The Soviet authorities in Leningrad had established a partisan headquarters on 27 September and despatched some 8,000 partisans to the rear of AGN in groups of 50 or so. The Leningrad partisan HQ had noted the welcome given to the Germans by the Balts and therefore specifically ordered the partisans that, as well as attacking the Germans, they should prioritise the re-establishment of the Party's influence and power in their operational zones. This latter objective was carried out in a most spectacular fashion by N. G. Vasilev's Second Partisan Brigade, which established itself in the Dno–Kholm–Staraia Russa triangle on the marshy left bank of the Lovat River, south of Lake Ilmen, an area of some 11,000sq km. During the twelve months of its existence, this Partisan *Krai* (a Soviet administrative area, often a border district) re-opened schools, clinics, Party offices and collective farms. Despite several attempts, the Dno *Krai* remained a thorn in AGN's side and a beacon of hope for the civilians in nearby areas under German control. So unsettling was it for the rear area of AGN that the 281st Security Division, unable to suppress it, on 4 November 1941 ordered 'large scale evacuations from the worst affected areas in order to avoid possible riots and epidemics'.

Another significant *Krai* was located in the rear of AGC in the vast, gloomy forests around Bryansk. The Germans estimated that by 1 January 1942 the partisans controlled some '8–10 *Raions* [a Soviet administrative area] comprising the Bryansk Agricultural Administrative Area'.

Similar *Krai* existed elsewhere such as that around Chernigov, less than 150km north-east of Kiev, where again forests and swamps along the Desna River provided excellent cover. However, these were isolated areas largely out of reach of the Red Army as it was marshalling its strength for the defence of Moscow.

AGC had launched Operation Typhoon with the aim of taking the Soviet capital and, so it was hoped in Berlin, ending the war. Unfortunately for the Germans, Typhoon spluttered to a halt within view of the Kremlin, and then the Soviets struck back.

The partisan contribution to the counter-offensive was not significant militarily but it did provide useful lessons in the arts of co-operation and co-ordination. Few of the partisan units had radios and were therefore unable to receive information and orders. Consequently, they limited themselves to sabotage and the harrying of small units and stragglers. Although relative pinpricks in terms of the damage done, it is important not to underestimate their effect on the morale of German troops undergoing their first major defeat of the war in the midst of the worst winter for decades – one for which they were ill-prepared. Retreating before ghost-like forces camouflaged and dressed for such arctic conditions, the men of AGC were individually and collectively prone to exaggerating the forces opposing them. Consequently, a single sniper became a platoon attacking, a sentry with his throat cut an all-out attack and a stray pony a full-scale cavalry attack with the accompanying cries of 'die Kosaken kommen' inducing further panic. Under orders from Hitler to stand firm and fight in conditions of limited winter light, with vehicles lacking fuel and anti-freeze and weapons too cold to handle, it is hardly surprising that the activities of the partisans were blown out of all proportion by those that believed they may have encountered them. In fact, General Franz Halder, Chief of the German General Staff until the autumn of 1942, wrote, 'the danger was exaggerated by the men, their nerves strained by the rapidly deteriorating situation at the front'.

Such was the critical nature of AGC's situation that on 30 December all security units were ordered to the front to plug the gaps, regardless of their capacity to carry out full-scale combat. Indeed, Police Battalion 307 assisted in holding off a Soviet ground and air attack on an airfield south-east of Vyazma. Its commander had gone into action, riding on a tank, shouting, 'Look here you swine you can't shoot German police.'

With the security and police units thus occupied the partisans had a prize opportunity to exploit. As January 1942 drew on Stalin aimed for the destruction of AGC. As part of a wide encircling movement I Guard Cavalry Corps, commanded by General P. A. Belov, was ordered to break through towards Vyazma and link up with paratroop units.

Unfortunately, Belov's combat troops broke through but not his artillery or supply echelons; nor did more than a tithe of the paratroopers make the drop accurately. Early in February Belov linked up with large partisan formations, some of which led the attack that liberated Dorogobuzh. In what was one of the earliest large-scale Red Army–partisan joint operations, co-ordinated by the Partisan Staff of the Kalinin Front ('Front' was the term applied to a Soviet Army Group), a gap in the German lines was made that became known as the Surazh Gate after the nearest town, Surazh, roughly 50km north-east of Vitebsk at the confluence of two marsh-straddled rivers. Many of the partisans were found to be regular soldiers who had been cut off behind enemy lines and these Belov pressed into the ranks, gaining some 2,400 replacements. The partisans led requisitioning parties and gathered fodder for the horses as well as food for the men. Furthermore, Belov was authorised to mobilise, as well as former soldiers, civilians up to the age of 45. Screening for possible collaborators and unreliable elements was carried out by the Special Induction Commission overseen by political officers.

However, Belov's mixed command of paratroopers, cavalrymen, partisans and other stragglers was under orders to relieve the remains of Thirty-Third Army, itself isolated behind the steadily firming German lines. Fighting to achieve this goal dragged on through March but, as the thaw became imminent, Stavka prepared one further push into AGC's rear to reinforce Belov. Belov suggested that his force breakout, leaving Dorogobuzh in partisan hands. This plan was rejected by Stalin, possibly for two reasons. First, there was an airfield in the town that had been used for re-supply flights from the 'Great Land' despite serious Luftwaffe interdiction, and NKVD and Party officials had been flown in and out and wounded troops evacuated. Secondly, if the army abandoned it, this would lower morale in the area. Unfortunately for Belov, the relief force was decimated by air and artillery strikes before its attack developed and the rump of Thirty-Third Army disintegrated. All that remained as a coherent fighting force were Belov's guardsmen and an increasing number of partisans. Nevertheless, this was not an insubstantial threat to the Germans who were forced to withdraw elements of 5th and 11th Panzer Divisions. The Germans were convinced that co-ordination and co-operation between the partisans and Moscow were much more highly organised than was in fact the case. Certainly, there was a degree of liaison across the front line but with the lack of communication equipment and the ghastliness of the weather, as well as the physical difficulties of linking up neatly, the Germans seem to have given the Soviets more credit than they were due.

Ensconced in and around Dorogobuzh Belov was ordered by Stavka to, 'report all you know about these partisan commanders, arrest all of them until the situation is clarified'. The 'situation' resulted in increasing suspicion in Moscow that some partisan bands were not under any form of control, were a cover for Red Army deserters or were merely armed brigands masquerading as patriots. It was the commanders of such groups that Moscow was keen to interview as everyone was aware of the 'Boss's' (Stalin) opinion of such rogue, buccaneering types that seemed to display all the worst characteristics of 'Partisanshchina'. All the partisan leaders that could be were rounded up and flown off to Moscow. Now Belov was faced with a dilemma as both he and his *Politruks* (unit political officers/commissars) had encouraged recruitment to and the activities of partisan formations, even imposing military structures and titles on them. To cast aspersions on several large groups of what were effectively heavily armed civilians, of possibly dubious loyalty, was not a step to be taken lightly given the military situation. However, nothing untoward happened and Belov's regular force returned to the Soviet main lines in June 1942, leaving behind a highly organised network of experienced partisan units. These formations would, as the weather improved, spread themselves across the forest arc and into the Pripet Marshes.

Difficult as the fighting had been in front of Moscow, it was the weather that had wreaked havoc amongst the less-well-organised or supplied partisan groups across the Little Land. Untold numbers of partisans, as well as others, died during that winter or faded back into the general population. Civilians had barely enough food for themselves after Axis administrators had taken their portion for military and home consumption. So, strong as they were in some areas, in others partisan units were non-existent.

As both Soviet and Axis high commands reviewed the situation both were in the process of formulating different approaches to security and partisan warfare.

Opposite top:
Patrolling the vast spaces in the rear areas was often more easily accomplished on horseback rather than in a vehicle. These men belong to the mounted section of a security division behind AGC. Their mounts appear to be in excellent condition, although the hardier local breeds were found to be more robust when the cold weather set in and were frequently the beasts of choice.

Opposite below:
As Operation Typhoon bogged down in first the mud and then the snow AGC's supply problems escalated. Here an Sd.Kfz 7 prime mover moves into position to haul supply lorries out of the morass. Such soft-skinned vehicles were easy prey for the partisans.

On 7 November the Red Army
marched through Red Square to
commemorate the Bolshevik takeover in
1917. The troops then marched directly
to the front. Stalin again broadcast to
the nation. The 'valiant men and women
guerrillas' were singled out for a special
mention alongside the regular armed
forces.

Soviet POWs taken during Operation
Typhoon by men of a panzer unit. It is
likely that they would have been left
where they were as the tanks forged
ahead. As one panzer corps report
noted, the men were 'too soft
concerning the natives ... officers often
demonstrated extreme carelessness
regarding the protection of troop
installations'.

Army Group Centre suffered over 100,000 casualties during Operation Typhoon and the subsequent Soviet winter offensive. Many of these were experienced veterans, men that it would be hard to replace. Although Soviet losses were heavier, they had re-occupied territory that would provide fresh recruits. Partisan formations re-united with the Great Country were usually immediately enrolled into the regular forces.

To the rear of Sixteenth Army (Army Group North) all communities were directed to take a census of the population in which non-locals were to be listed with the date of their arrival. Such lists would be checked by means of snap roll calls. Non-compliance would result in 'collective punitive measures'.

As they retreated the men of Army Group Centre destroyed any buildings that could have afforded shelter to the advancing Soviet troops. Inevitably, this created hardship for the civilians and again provided cause for them to take up arms. A partisan veteran remembered finding a German corpse wearing items of female clothing including a bra to protect his ears and face. He noted a sense of satisfaction and pity.

It was not only the Germans who destroyed property. Here a partisan unit can be seen evacuating a village prior to leading the inhabitants through the lines. The buildings are just beginning to burn to deny the enemy shelter. The original caption notes this scene as taking place 'near the Surazh Gate, Feb 1942'.

The Germans were still mainly a horse-drawn army. However, as thousands of draught animals died during the first winter in the USSR, local horses and *panje* wagons were pressed into service. These wagons are carrying supplies for the SS Cavalry Brigade which was engaged, and nearly destroyed, at the front near Peno at the junction of AGN and AGC during January 1942.

One of the partisan units attached to Belov's command during early 1942 was the 1st Smolensk Partisan Division. In a short time it would grow to a force of over 7,000 men with 2 light tanks, 10 pieces of artillery and 50 mortars. Here three of the division's Model 1932 45mm anti-tank guns, liberally smeared with whitewash camouflage paint, are seen.

Urban partisan operations were much more restricted due to the vicious nature of the retaliation meted out by the occupation forces. Nevertheless, they were undertaken during the early days particularly. One of the most dramatic episodes was the destruction of the Kreshchatik Avenue in Kiev on 24 September 1941. The city's occupation HQ was destroyed, as was the German officers' club. The bombing was believed to have been the work of an NKVD unit led by I. D. Kudyra, who was captured and executed in 1942.

Five days after the Kiev bombings the first round-ups of Jews were announced in Kiev. Between 29 and 30 September over 33,000 Jews were executed by men of Einsatzgruppen C, 2 German police battalions and Ukrainian collaborators. It was a horrific portent of life in the Little Land of the occupied territories. During the next two years the Babi Yar ravine witnessed the murder of thousands of POWs, Jews, Communists and other ethnically and politically undesirable groups.

One ethnic minority favoured by the occupation administration was the Crimean Tartars. This group had suffered considerable hardship during the twenty years of Soviet rule in Crimea and was generally violently anti-Communist. Although many joined the partisans in the Yalai Hills and the Red Army, some 3,000 enrolled in Axis security units.

Amongst the forests and lakes of the Karelian Front the Finns and Soviet partisan bands played out a vicious game of cat and mouse. With a tiny population of Russians, the partisans were generally formed around NKVD Frontier Guard units that were well versed in the terrain and smuggler's routes in this wilderness. Here a Finnish soldier poses for the camera during an anti-partisan sweep.

The most significant nationalist movement was in Ukraine, and was particularly strong west and north-west of the Dnieper River. Several rival groups had existed pre-war but these coalesced into one led by S. A. Bandera with a military organisation known as the UPA (the Ukrainian Insurgent Army). On 30 June 1941 the nationalists occupied Lvov pre-empting the Germans who, on arrival, dispersed the embryonic government. Here natives of Lvov deface images of Russian politicians.

Another significant problem in establishing an urban partisan movement was the destruction in towns and cities behind Axis lines. L. P. Kazinets, who attempted to set up partisan groups in Minsk, commented, 'we have tried several times to set up a Party group which could carry out mass agitation work amongst the population . . . the work goes ahead in bits and pieces'. Most of the population was too busy finding shelter and surviving.

A fallen idol. For many millions in the occupied lands the new regime had to be lived with regardless of politics. For them the Great Land was far away.

Politics aside, the strength of simple patriotism should not be underestimated. The Russians were, and are, deeply attached to the *Rodina* (Motherland) despite its shortcomings and were prepared to fight for it, a feeling encouraged by the Communist Party. The flag of Belov's I Guard Cavalry Corps was a symbol of this newly resurrected emotional appeal.

Hitler, left, talks to two members of a *Reichsarbeitdienst* (State National Work Service, RAD), battalion number 321 from the Saar district. RAD units supported the army by repairing and building roads, airfields and other essential infrastructure. By 1942 over 400 RAD formations were working on the Eastern Front. When the situation demanded they were expected to fight to defend their sites from partisans and the Red Army.

Stalin's mistrust of any organisation perceived to be out of the state's control was such that he took particular interest in the activities of the partisan movement. He viewed their primary task as being to, 're-establish the organs of state power in the village, resume the normal activity of the collective farms and exterminate German agents and traitors'.

Chapter Four

Body Counts

During the Soviet winter offensive Second Panzer Army (General Rudolph Schmidt succeeded Guderian on 25 December 1941) had been driven back to a line between Orel and Kursk. With his rear insecure and supply lines threatened by partisans, Schmidt, with permission from Rosenberg's Ostministerium and AGC's HQ, set in train the expansion of what became known as the Autonomous Administrative District of Lokot, 75km south of Bryansk with the town of Lokot as its capital. The first Russian leader was killed in an engagement with partisans and was replaced by his deputy, B. V. Kaminski, who rapidly increased the size of the anti-partisan militia. Kaminski was appointed mayor of the region and commander of the militia, which undertook anti-partisan operations on an increasingly ambitious scale. The collective-farm system was abolished and a relatively free economy was introduced. As the area, larger than Belgium, began to flourish it attracted immigrants from neighbouring districts and the population expanded to over 1 million. These refugees frequently declared themselves to be unsympathetic to Stalinism and living in fear of the partisans. The militia was often used alongside German units in an anti-partisan role and gained a reputation for ferocity and ruthlessness. It was converted into the Russian National Liberation Army in 1943. A similar form of mini civil war was also beginning in Ukraine where nationalist partisans were fighting Communist Party, NKVD and other partisan groups. Initially, the Ukrainian Nationalists had hoped that the Axis would allow some form of autonomy for Ukraine. However, only words and token gestures were forthcoming from Berlin and the Ukrainians took matters into their own hands, although avoided combat with Axis forces.

Nor were these the only collaborationist forces to be used in such a manner. During the autumn of 1941 approval had been given to each army group to raise Cossack formations to supplement their security forces. As with the other Schuma formations, the bulk of the recruits were recruited from POW camps.

The security of Axis rear areas was now assuming considerably more importance than had been anticipated a year earlier. The simple reason for that was the fact that the war with the USSR was not over, the Wehrmacht had failed and the campaign would last at least another summer. Consequently, a considerable degree of re-evaluation was necessary.

The basis of anti-partisan operations were the Barbarossa Directives, supplemented in July and September by instructions that, 'We take … Drastic means in order to crush the movement [partisan] in the shortest possible time . . . a deterrent effect can be attained only by unusual severity, the death penalty for 50–100 Communists should generally be regarded in those cases as suitable atonement for one German soldier's life'. Attempts to moderate this, such as the taking of hostages, were made but these had little effect as reports were reaching senior staff in the Wehrmacht, the SS and the police noting hundreds of instances of partisan activity across the occupied territories. Such events led to a succession of locally issued deterrent measures. As the HSSPF for the rear of AGC, Erich von Dem Bach-Zelewski, commented, 'since orders proved insufficient a wild state of anarchy resulted in all anti-partisan operations'. Confusion existed about who killed who for what reason, be it the Einsatzgruppen slaughtering Jews, Communists and commissars, security troops and the police alongside local forces killing armed partisans, suspected partisans or children collecting munitions from the old battlefields or regular soldiers hanging and shooting 'Persons found wandering in streets after dark or found near rail or highway bridges at any time'. It still meant the killing of civilians, partisans or not, on a massive scale. As many as 800 inhabitants of Kiev were 'shot as a reprisal for acts of sabotage' and '50 male inhabitants shot as reprisal measures (in Simferopol, Crimea) for the German soldier killed', as reported by AGS. As an order of Third Panzer Army stated, 'the [partisan] bands must be exterminated in combat. Any methods are permissible and imply in any case exemption from punishment for the personnel ordered into action against bands'. This carte blanche to kill was thus reinforced in early 1942. At roughly the same time, February 1942, the army's senior security warfare officer, General Max von Schenckendorf, issued a report entitled, 'Proposals for the Liquidation of the Partisans'. What the general asked for were more native troops for security duties, something which Hitler was unlikely to approve. On 10 February the Führer had ordered that 'no further native combat units were to be organised by the Army for anti-partisan work'. Furthermore, all such units were to become the responsibility of the HSSPF and so part of Himmler's empire. However, native units could still be recruited for Schuma battalions in the Reichskommisariats, again part of the Reichsführer's purview. Meanwhile, the SS had analysed the partisans' methodology, particularly their practice of 'hit and move on to another area' to avoid counter-attack. As space was not at a premium the partisans could avoid pursuit by melting away into the almost trackless forests. Therefore, Himmler concluded that extermination was preferable to capturing and holding ground. The army generally took the opposite view.

Whilst the assessment and discussion continued in Berlin and elsewhere, out in the marshes and forests the anti-partisan sweeps were growing in complexity and scale. One such exercise, Operation Munich, in the Yelna–Dorogobuzh area began on 19 March and lasted for over two weeks. On paper this was one of the largest of the war as it involved two panzer and one security division, although in the event only the latter took an active part. Yelna was recaptured but Dorogobuzh remained in partisan hands. The 10th Panzer Division reported, 'the roads are heavily mined . . . It would appear that the partisans are constantly reinforced by airborne troops.' At about the same time, further to the west and south of Bobruisk, a similar sweep, Operation Bamberg, was underway, involving 707th Infantry Division, a Slovakian infantry regiment and German Police Battalion 315. The tactics used would set the pattern for subsequent operations which would be divided into four phases:

1. Marching up and forming a great cauldron (encirclement) with a diameter of 25–30km.
2. Tightening the encirclement, gradually reducing the area.
3. The 'clearing of the cauldron' as it became smaller.
4. The 'mopping up' by 'repeated thorough cleaning and crossing of the area in a backwards direction up to the second initial position'. During this process villages and farms within the inner zone would be destroyed along with their inhabitants.

During the latter phase food and equipment would be removed. This conformed to one of the tasks outlined before the operation began which was the annihilation of the partisan bands, pacification of the countryside and the collection of grain and livestock. The interrogation of villagers was undertaken by members of the Secret Field Police.

Bamberg ran from 26 March to 6 April, during which time the official German body count was 3,500, of whom roughly 50 per cent were partisans. Soviet sources estimate the number killed as more than 4,300. A total of 47 rifles and sub-machine guns were captured for Axis losses of 7 dead and 15 wounded. Although Schenckendorf praised the commander of 707th Infantry Division on 'having annihilated 3,000 partisans', the operation was not considered particularly successful. The economic authorities were not impressed at the small number of livestock rounded up or the paltry 115 tons of grain and 120 tons of potatoes removed. Interestingly, these officials had suggested to the military that they should not remove the peasants' seed grain or their last cows lest such moves led to a 'deterioration of the mood of the population'. What the mood of the surviving population was went unrecorded.

As the weather improved both partisans and the occupation forces stepped up their activities. AGS was to carry out an offensive to secure the oilfields of the

Caucasus, which it was believed would result in the defeat of the Soviet Union. The offensive was to be known as Operation Blue. To replace the losses suffered during the previous summer Hitler had coerced his allies, Italy, Hungary and Romania, to increase their forces on the Eastern Front, where they would be committed to the summer offensive in the south. However, prior to the commencement of Operation Blue, it was decided that, 'the entire length of the line . . . was to be reformed . . . and the rear area mopped up immediately after the close of the "Muddy Season" [the thaw of March to May]'. This obviously meant that the partisans threatening the railway lines were to be dealt with by a series of security sweeps.

AGN carried out a number of small-scale operations on its section of the Dno–Novosokolniki line that connected it with AGC. The subsequent report stated, 'it is under nominal German control . . . open to interdiction along its entire length'. Communications with AGC were, 'exceedingly tenuous'. Although the security troops were successful in driving the partisans out of swept areas, the success was transient as they often reappeared within a few days at a different spot on the railway. However, it was AGC that was faced with the most pressing problems as it was important to Operation Blue that lines of supply from the central area were maintained. Consequently, Operation Birdsong was launched with the express intention of clearing the Bryansk forests of partisan groups and securing the road and rail links.

Following the established encirclement format, on 5 June, two infantry regiments supported by a panzer regiment committed over 5,000 men against a partisan force estimated to be less than half that number. The Germans counted 2,600 partisan casualties and 500 men of military age arrested and a further 12,000 civilians evacuated against their own 189 casualties. Although apparently wiped out, the partisans simply moved elsewhere and it was clear that Stalin was perfectly happy to accept such a rate of attrition.

Opposite top:
It was men such as these that joined the militia in the Lokot district. Such a relatively large collaborationist organisation as this can hardly have escaped the ears of Stalin's intelligence services and fuelled his fears of this type of arrangement spreading.

Opposite below:
Part of a Cossack security *sotnia* (unit of 100), raised from POWs. The experiment using them began in October 1941 and was approved by Hitler the following month due to the success of such formations. They were to be 'adequately armed, mounted, clothed, paid and fed, and given missions against the partisans in definite areas under the command of their own officers'. The colour of the trouser stripe denoted the region from which they came.

When the Soviet bureaucracy was evacuated or fled the resultant interregnum was often filled by locally elected groups that strove to keep law and order. This situation led to the establishment of the Lokot administration. With the arrival of the invaders the initial wave of soldiers usually left such bodies in place. But as 286th Security Division (AGC) reported, 'Considerable trust was placed in village elders and mayors who were often informed of impending anti-partisan sweeps and often passed the information to irregular groups.'

Potential recruits for the Schuma battalions. Recruitment was aimed at the non-Russian ethnic groups, such as these Asiatic Red Army POWs. Kazakhs, Uzbeks and Turkmen were amongst those enrolled. They would be given badges to wear on their old Soviet uniforms to identify their status and were generally issued with Soviet weaponry.

German security troops cluster around the radio waiting for new orders during Operation Marsh Fever in early 1942. The gruesome body count for this action totalled 389 partisans killed, 1,274 suspects shot and 8,350 Jews liquidated. As Bach-Zelewski's testimony at the Nuremberg Trials recorded, 'the fight against partisans was gradually used as an excuse to carry out other measures, such as the extermination of Jews and gypsies . . . and the terrorisation of civilians by shooting and looting'.

Himmler, interpreting Hitler's desires, required the reduction of the Slavic population in the east by some 30–40,000,000 people to ensure Lebensraum (living space) for the Aryan resettlement of the region. At the end of each security operation meticulous records of the dead, categorised according to type including 'partisans' and 'Jews', were always drawn up and submitted to the relevant authorities.

Unable to recruit sufficient local manpower, AGC resorted to transferring two brigades of Hungarian security troops from AGS. Ill-equipped, newly conscripted and poorly trained, these brigades behaved so badly, indulging in widespread looting and indiscriminate killing, that the locals were rapidly turned from neutral to pro-partisan in their sympathies.

As the realities of Axis occupation became clear the people under German rule in the Little Land slowly came to terms with life. Soviet propaganda regarding the ill-treatment of civilians was almost daily proved to be fact. Shortages of food and other commodities were continual and the often-casual brutality of the occupiers contributed to a growing feeling of dissatisfaction and encouraged recruitment to the partisans.

To provide food for the Reich and the Wehrmacht on the Eastern Front peasant farmers were still tied to the collective-farm system of the USSR. Despite rumours and unofficial pronouncements, the new regime had not allowed widespread private ownership of the land. Thousands of officials were drafted in to supervise the collection of supplies. In Berlin the controversial topic of how to treat the Slavs continued to be debated as memos suggesting they be treated less harshly to ensure co-operation were regularly looked at and generally dismissed.

Joseph Goebbels, Hitler's propaganda minister, congratulates a senior railway official on his bravery award for duties on the Eastern Front. Goebbels noted in his diary, 'Partisans have blasted the railway tracks in the central front between Bryansk and Roslavl at five points – a further proof of their extremely discomforting activity.'

On 11 March 1942 AGC gained a special squadron of obsolete aircraft, such as this Henschel Hs 126, specifically tasked with anti-partisan duties. Although it only carried a bomb load of 150kg, the 126 was to prove its worth during many anti-partisan sweeps.

Lightly armed with MP40 sub-machine guns, members of a security division patrol for the camera in terrain typical of the forests where the partisans operated. Fighting in such a landscape meant the rate of fire was usually more important than accuracy as shards of bark could prove as lethal as bullets, magnifying the effect of the thirty-two-round magazine considerably.

The Red Air Force operated a fleet of aircraft to supply the partisans and evacuate the wounded. The U-2s/Po-2 seen here was specifically built as an air ambulance. Ruggedly constructed, the U-2 was ideally suited for the rough and ready landings it often had to make on extemporised airfields behind enemy lines.

Aircraft evacuation was rarely available. In the event of pursuit wounded partisans often committed suicide to avoid capture.

A Belorussian partisan armed with a Mosin-Nagant rifle, the Red Army's standard weapon, and sporting a well-filled cartridge belt, looks warily into the lens. Such middle-aged men were often veterans of the First World War and the Russian Civil War. Accustomed to living a very simple life, these men made good recruits for the partisans.

Inland from any naval base, such as Sevastopol, a partisan unit was likely to include sailors, such as this cheerful young man. As with recruits from the army, these men brought a sense of discipline and weapons experience with them.

As part of the precautions now being taken all railway lines in the occupied territories had the foliage to a distance of more than 100m removed to prevent ambush. Regular patrolling was carried out by security forces. A considerable percentage of the Soviet rail network was single track, as can be seen here.

But away from the railways it had become necessary to provide escorts, such as this Panzer II, for supply convoys along routes that were known to be prone to partisan attacks.

To improve security along the railways the Germans employed armoured trains, pressing into service captured Soviet rolling stock such as the locomotive seen here. The guns would provide artillery support for the ground troops and clearly their mobility was a great asset.

With the attention of the Wehrmacht focused on the activities of AGS and the upcoming campaign to capture the oil fields of the Caucasus, there were those in both Moscow and Berlin who were interested in the reaction of the population, particularly the mountain tribes (seen here), several of which had been in revolt against Soviet rule for some time. Nor were the Don or Kuban Cossacks, the lands of which lay in the path of the Axis offensive, filled with loyalty to Stalin.

Chapter Five

CHQPM

The partisan movement that had developed since the summer of 1941 was a many faceted organisation, answerable to a variety of masters or in some cases none. The structure, where it existed, was haphazard with little formality in the way many of the groups operated. With the Red Army, the NKVD and the Communist Party all having partisan formations of their own, it became clear that a structure had to be imposed upon them if they were to achieve significant success. At first the members of the units were volunteers, mainly Communists, from the urban centres or isolated groups of Red Army men. The latter, it was estimated in early 1942, comprised over 60 per cent of the total. But, due to the winter's severity as much as to the activities of the Axis, thousands of these original fighters died or made their way back to the Great Land. Those who remained behind had to replace their losses and to do this Moscow introduced conscription into the occupied territories in the following way.

> All members of the Armed Forces who escaped … and are at home, also men of the class of 1925 report to your units or join the partisans. Those who remain in hiding and continue to sit at home in order to save their skins and those who do not join the patriotic war to help destroy the German robbers, also those who desert to the Fascist army and help the latter to carry on a robber war against the Soviet people, are traitors to the homeland and will be liquidated by us sooner or later.

The wording is interesting as it offers no alternative to draft dodgers but death. Furthermore, as well as raising recruits it was also an attempt to reassert Soviet authority. Nor was it merely the 17-year-olds but everyone up to the age of 50 that was expected to answer the call, unless physically or mentally unable to serve. Useful a tool as conscription was, it proved to be a mixed blessing. The majority of the recruits had no training, lacked discipline and were concerned for the fate of their families left behind at the mercy of the occupation authorities. Often they were suspected, as they had not joined up earlier, of Fascist sympathies and collaborationist tendencies. Consequently, their every move was watched until they proved themselves reliable and only then would they be armed. Unsurprisingly, the morale of such men was low. Reports of these feelings found their way back to Moscow and when such were considered alongside news of soldiers deserting, collaborationist police and security units and unrest in the northern Caucasus it was decided that a single body would oversee the partisan movement. It would enforce the orders that had been issued since the invasion, direct operations, co-ordinate supply and propaganda efforts and, in short, control the partisans and thereby claw back authority over the population and wage a more organised war behind enemy lines.

On 30 May 1942 the GKO (State Committee for Defence) issued a directive that activated the Central Head Quarters of the Partisan Movement (CHQPM). Its principal responsibilities were to be 'to maintain reliable communication with partisan formations, co-ordinate their activities, organise co-operation between Red Army units and partisan formations, generalise and propagate partisan warfare experience, supply units with weapons, ammunition, medical supplies and other means of logistic support, train qualified personnel for partisan units and transport personnel into the enemy rear'.

Consisting of three departments, Operations, Intelligence and Security, the CHQPM was based in Moscow. The Operations Department planned and co-ordinated important political and military raids, analysed reports, evaluated the general situation and prepared maps and particular orders for larger partisan formations. When necessary they would provide specialist personnel to support a mission. Intelligence planned and co-ordinated missions in co-operation with the Red Army and NKVD. The Security Department was particularly concerned with counter-espionage and the detection of enemy agents in partisan units or decoy partisan units established by the Germans to confuse Moscow and the civilian population. This latter was not as widespread as the Soviets believed due to the Germans' problems recruiting so-called V-Men (*Vertrauensmanner* – trusties or informers).

The original organisational basis of the partisan movement had been geo-politically based on the boundaries of the constituent republics of the USSR and their internal regions (*oblasts*) right down to district level. As such areas did not correspond with the Red Army's fronts (a group of armies named geographically), this could result in confusion of command and control and intelligence gathering. For example, one front could be operating across the boundaries of several *oblasts* in maybe the Ukrainian, Belarusian or Russian Republics. To avoid such complications the CHQPM retained the original system already in place.

However, the Ukrainian partisan organisation and its Moldavian (Transnistria) sub-branch still reported directly to the Soviet High Command. Republic and lower level partisan headquarters and staffs were responsible to the Party equivalents. As a result of this the Red Army's partisan planning and organisational bureaux were disbanded but, from September 1942, the CHQPM had representation on each front's military council. Irregular and regular forces co-ordination would be led by the CHQPM.

At the head of the CHQPM was its Chief of Staff, P. K. Ponomarenko, the head of the Belorussian Communist Party. But at his side was V. T. Sergienko of the NKVD. The latter reported to L. P. Beria, the commissar who led the NKVD with direct access to Stalin and a man similar to Himmler inasmuch as he was devoted to empire building and the expansion of his own power base. As one who revelled in sniffing out deviation from the Party line, keeping a close watch on such a potentially difficult group as the partisans would have given him much satisfaction.

The CHQPM began immediately to enforce the structure of its administration from top to bottom. However, achieving this depended on communications; nevertheless, it was soon claiming oversight of more than 600 partisan formations.

The training of specialists was a hugely important function of the CHQPM and to this end several partisan schools were established in and around Moscow. The curriculum included parachuting, scouting and intelligence gathering, communications, propaganda, demolitions and medical skills. Veterans described themselves as 'city boys' unused to foraging for food, building smokeless fires and identifying edible plants in the forests and marshes where they would be operating. In 1941 training had been quite low key but twelve months later it had stepped up a gear. As the NKVD already had such schools these were expanded. Graduates from these 'partisan academies' were then dropped, airlifted or walked in to join their formations where their proficiency often meant the difference between life and death. As the CHQPM developed its activities during the summer of 1942, Stalin called a conference where he was joined by the commanders and commissars of all the major partisan units in Belorussia, Ukraine and the Orel and Smolensk *oblasts*. The conference was held in Moscow and resulted in an order from the 'Boss' entitled 'Concerning the Missions of the Partisan Movement'. This document restated the point that the partisan movement was an 'All people's struggle', which was an attempt to unify all the non-Russian elements of the USSR's population.

Furthermore, emphasis was placed on demolition work aimed specifically at the railways. In order to achieve this, new types of mines and explosive devices were created for partisan use. Co-operation with the Red Army was highlighted and the potential of the partisan movement was quoted as being 'One of the decisive factors in [achieving] victory.' For the vast majority of the partisans who attended this conference it was an awe-inspiring experience. Possibly it was their first visit to Moscow and certainly the only time they were likely to move amongst such powerful figures. There is no doubt that it would have been inspirational for the less cynical, who, it was hoped, would return to their units full of tales to tell and boasts to make about mingling, drinking and smoking with Comrade Stalin. It is unlikely that Stalin would have let slip the opportunity to weigh up his field commanders and it is probably correct to assume that more than one did not match up to his critical appraisal.

The NKVD was equally active during this period. Concerned over the lack of partisan activity across Ukraine at a time when the Axis was rapidly advancing into the Caucasus, towards the Volga River and Voronezh, it stepped up its operations.

The partisan unit, part of the NKVD's Special Purposes Rifle Brigade, known as the 'Winners' and led by a veteran, rather roguish NKVD officer, D. N. Medvetsev, was dispatched to Ukraine. The purpose of the mission was to assassinate the Reichskommisar for Ukraine Erich Koch. Of lesser importance were the tasks of demolition, sabotage and recruitment, as well as 'showing the flag' and reminding the population that the Soviet Union was still undefeated. Koch had chosen to establish his capital in the western Ukrainian city of Rovno rather than Kiev.

Amongst this group was Albert Tsessarsky, who has provided much of the information detailed here regarding this mission. A section of the unit was flown into the Briansk *oblast* on 10 June 1942, where it prepared an airstrip into which the remaining seventy partisans were flown. They made their way on foot south-westwards into Ukraine, where they were engaged by the Germans for the first time. They fought their way out of encirclement at a cost of one dead and four wounded. Tsessarsky remembered they were 'very excited and enthusiastic' following their first victory. However, it was necessary to travel swiftly and carefully as the Germans were now aware of their presence and 'country life' was proving very difficult for these city boys to adapt to. The group included a professional footballer and 'well-known boxer N. F. Korolov'.

By October they were nearing Rovno, some 200km west of Kiev. At this point they were joined by one of the most heroic (in post-war Soviet partisan pantheon) figures of the partisan movement, N. I. Kuznetsov, a 31-year-old NKVD officer who was actually to carry out Koch's assassination. With the pieces in place it only remained to carry out the job.

One partisan veteran, Boris Chorny, on learning of the outbreak of war, volunteered for the NKVD Special Brigade. After many problems he then volunteered for Medvedev's formation and again faced difficulties. He quipped during an interview in 2003, 'It was so hard to get the opportunity to die for your Motherland.' This was not the case, certainly in the field, a few months later.

New recruits to a partisan unit listen to their new commander and the group's political commissar. At first they would be allocated menial tasks and undergo vetting procedures. If the unit had a radio then a call to Moscow might be made to verify the newcomer's credentials. All partisan formations were very security conscious, fearing German agents might infiltrate the membership.

The Germans were not the only ones to tolerate religion in the Soviet Union. Stalin had already summoned up the heroes of Russia's past wars, such a Bagration and Suvorov, in an attempt to invoke patriotic as well as Communist motivation. During Easter 1942 religious practice once more became acceptable across the USSR.

A reconstruction of a partisan winter shelter, a *zemlyanka*, shows how well-prepared partisans would have lived during the winter. With its earth roof just above ground and its timber-clad walls surrounded by soil, such a dugout provided warmth and shelter for many partisan groups. If well camouflaged, these huts proved difficult to find. There was usually a concealed second exit in case of discovery.

A radio operator in the field. In fact, the majority of operators were women. Such specialists were protected at all costs to ensure continuity of contact with higher authority and were also not allowed to hand over their radios to another operator. A change of operator often flagged up problems in Moscow, maybe due to a possible mistake in coded call signs. German intelligence agencies monitored partisan frequencies hoping for information on their plans or simply interjecting to cause confusion and sow mistrust. Just over 10 per cent of the 600 units in touch with the CHQPM during the summer of 1942 had radios.

The structure of partisan formations mirrored that of the army. This man is 'the Chief of Staff Barykina' of a unit operating near Gomel. The commander (a rank in itself) and his political officer were the senior figures who led and planned operations. Often called brigades, the formations were usually named after a personality, the region in which they operated or adopted a slogan such as 'For Victory and Liberation'.

Supplies from the Great Land, including artillery shells, are stockpiled in one of the partisan *krai* around Bryansk. Light artillery was not an unusual asset for some of the larger formations, but ammunition re-supply was often problematic. In cases of surprise attack the guns were often left behind.

To spread news of victories and atrocities newspapers and leaflets were printed in Moscow for distribution in the Little Land or the Temporarily Occupied Territories. One such, the *Partisan*, is seen here.

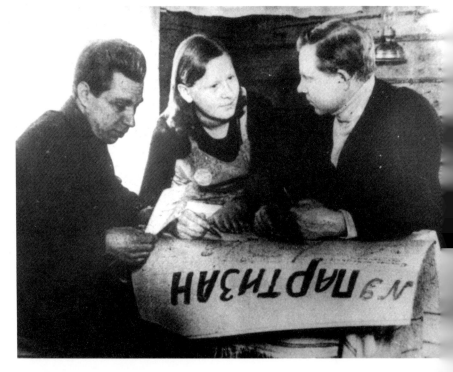

A trio of partisan scouts leaves on a mission. The scouts specialised in observation and intelligence gathering ahead of the main body of the unit. Patience and excellent field-craft were their stock in trade, as well as observational skills. Often it was an onerous task to gather food supplies and meant negotiating with locals, who were often terrified in case they were dealing with disguised Schuma troops.

On the left a Cossack member of a security unit with a German soldier and his muzzled police dog. Such collaborators would deal ruthlessly with any partisan who fell into their hands and vice versa. Little quarter was given or expected.

On the right of this image is the partisan leader S. A. Kovpak, a Ukrainian partisan commander. He was promoted to general by Stalin during the conference of September 1942. Stalin said then, 'The most important thing is to maintain stronger links with the people.' Here Kovpak is seen with members of his staff.

During the time it was behind the lines Medvedev's group witnessed, according to Albert Tsessarsky, 'eight weddings and one divorce, all carried out with Medvedev's approval. A pie would be baked and placed on the stump of a tree, the couple came forward and Medvedev plus his aide would perform the ceremony.' However, extra-marital relations were frowned upon as bad for discipline. But as Boris Chorny remembered, 'Love is love, women got pregnant.'

The first in a remarkable trio of images. The man on the right is one of two collaborators. Here he is undergoing interrogation by a member of the partisan staff who appears to be less than fascinated. The prisoner's body language indicates high anxiety and the need to justify himself.

The collaborators are brought before the entire unit to hear sentence pronounced. Whilst three guards keep their eyes on the accused, the rest listen with rapt attention to their commander's words. It is likely the audience included the witnesses or victims of the collaborators' crime and possibly family members.

Sentence having been pronounced, in the name of the Soviet government, the condemned men dug their own grave and awaited the executioner's shots. Such events were, when time and circumstances permitted, carried out with sombre formality. Soviet law was adhered to, justice seen to be done and retribution swift and merciless. Naturally, news of such events was carried far and wide purposely to discourage collaboration.

German executions were often carried out in a more public fashion, such as outside this confectioner's shop. The amount of time that corpses were left hanging was not specified. The placard declares the reason for the executions.

Villagers in the foothills of the Caucasus Mountains gather around a German half-track as an officer takes sightings. In many such areas Axis troops received a positive reception. The plans for the occupation were intended to be more lenient than elsewhere in the USSR as the people were regarded as racially superior to the Slavs.

Concerns about the loyalty of the Caucasian peoples were not without foundation, as this image demonstrates. A senior officer of German mountain troops is cordially received by a local dignitary with the traditional bread and salt. A further gift seems to be awaiting presentation. The interpreter, closest to the camera at right, is a member of a German unit of Caucasian troops.

Almost the farthest and certainly the highest point of Axis penetration into the Caucasus was Mount Elbruz, scaled by German mountain troops on 21 August 1942. Hitler was less than impressed with this display of their skill. Mountain troops proved adept at anti-partisan warfare when deployed in this role due to their light equipment and use of pack animals.

A ragged Soviet poster decorates the wall of a burned out building in a recently liberated town following the Axis defeat at Stalingrad. The civilians to the bottom left are reading posted sheets of *Pravda*, the Soviet newspaper. Once again under Stalin, they would have to demonstrate the innocence of their activities during the period of occupation.

Chapter Six

Kovpak, Koch and Kuznetsov

Dressed as a German supply officer, with papers in the name of Lieutenant Paul Siebart, a German of Baltic extraction, as noted in his Wehrmacht soldier's book, Kuznetsov prepared for his mission. He spent each evening closeted with Tsessarsky, who hoped to improve his German. However, Siebart did not have the correct movement orders and consequently these had to be forged. A German typewriter and blank forms were therefore stolen. With these, Tsessarsky, 'with my knowledge of German typed out' what was required. A rubber stamp was created, in two days, by another member of the unit and the completed document was signed illegibly by Medvedev's political officer. Kuznetsov was escorted to the outskirts of Rovno where, 'He was saluted by two guards and allowed to pass.' From then on the 'Winners' settled into a routine. They traversed the region carrying out various acts of sabotage and retaliation, as well as establishing contact with other groups and bringing them under the control of the CHQPM. Inevitably, the unit took casualties and replacements were flown in from the Great Land, as well as recruited locally. Moscow also provided a cine camera and operator to record their activities for posterity. Many of the new arrivals were foreigners, Communist refugees. Tsessarsky noted thirteen nationalities under Medvedev's command. Included amongst them were Bulgarians, Balts, Poles, Czechs and at least one Spaniard, Africa de las Heras Gavilan, described as 'a heroic scout'. During this time they, with the aid of Kuznetsov, were able to discover the location of Hitler's forward HQ at Vinnitsa in Ukraine, known as 'Werewolf', which had been completed in April 1942. Over 4,000 Soviet POWs had been involved in its construction and, along with more than 200 inhabitants of a nearby village, they had been executed to prevent its whereabouts becoming widely known and the subject of partisan attacks. No partisan raid was mounted on 'Werewolf' and it was destroyed during the German retreat from the area in 1944. Other information relayed to Moscow via the Winners related to troop movements from the west to support the operation to relieve the Sixth Army in Stalingrad, the build-up of forces for Operation Citadel, the German offensive at Kursk during July 1943, and the plan to assassinate Stalin, Roosevelt and Churchill during the Teheran conference in 1943.

Despite his thorough preparations, Kuznetsov, code named 'Fluff', was not able to kill Koch. However, he did carry out several assassinations during the course of 1943 in Rovno and Lvov. The method did not vary. Dressed in German uniform, he would approach his target, pronounce sentence and then shoot them.

Boris Chorny, a fellow member of the Winners and a friend of Tsessarky's from Moscow, described 'every day life as fighting' and that operating in the western Ukraine was really dangerous 'due to the activities of the Bandera men [Ukrainian nationalists]' who 'cause more casualties than combat with the Germans'. Rarely did they stay in the same place for more than a week.

Caring for casualties was one of Tsessarsky's responsibilities as he had been in his final year at medical school before joining up. He remembered the lack of medical supplies, which, unless they could be captured, was always critical. Bandages were made from parachute silk and 'grass and other unconventional medicines were used, on the advice of local women well-versed in such things'. After he had lost his surgical equipment in a marsh fight, Tsessarsky was forced to amputate a comrade's leg to prevent the spread of gangrene, 'A two-handed saw was altered and used, the man was carried for the rest of the war and survived – vodka was used as an anaesthetic.' Understandably, the patient cursed a lot during the procedure. This was something Medvedev disapproved of, viewing it as the thin end of the wedge that could lead to the erosion of discipline. Indeed, the Winners were expected to keep themselves and their clothing clean, particularly their collars, and to shave regularly. Obviously, this was a sensible precaution given the conditions they were living and fighting in, but it was also to prove wrong the German propaganda that described them as 'dirty, unshaved wild men and forest thieves'.

Looting and excessive drinking were also regarded as breaches of discipline. Mild forms of punishment included grinding corn; harsher punishments were related to the crimes, for example, looting was punishable by death. Indeed, Chorny had initially been rejected by Medvedev as he appeared to be 'undisciplined'. On probation until he proved himself in his first action, Chorny served with the Winners as a scout. One of his responsibilities was to maintain contact with Kuznetsov, either meeting him or receiving messages by courier.

Both veterans spoke highly of Medvedev, 'a romantic . . . possessed a great sense of humour'. Tsessarsky, aged 7, had heard him speak in Odessa prior to Medvedev's first of three dismissals from the NKVD. Despite this, he remained a convinced Communist. According to Tsessarsky, Medvedev, 'Sent a telegram to Stalin criticising the NKVD in which he wrote, I'm on hunger strike under your statue by the Kursk railway station in Moscow.' Recalled to Moscow in July 1941, he was sent behind German lines where his unit was responsible for kidnapping Prince Lvov, the son of a prominent politician under the Tsar and leader of the Provisional Government in 1917. Lvov had been lined up by the Germans to be the token Russian governor of Moscow. The manner in which Medvedev behaved made him the embodiment of much that Stalin distrusted about the partisan leadership, *Partisanshchina*, a sense of independence, charisma and the like that were essential in the leaders of partisan formations. However, his record of success was clearly matched by an increase in discretion as he survived Stalin's reign, was made a Hero of the Soviet Union and retired as a colonel to pursue a literary career.

But Medvedev's was not the only significant partisan unit operating west of the Dnieper River between 1942 and 1944. In early 1943 Chorny and his scouting section were ordered to make contact with a party of S. A. Kovpak's partisans. Reaching the appointed spot, but uncertain of the identity of the other group, Chorny and his men began to exchange abuse and slang with them. Having thus developed a degree of mutual trust, both sides emerged. Chorny offered himself as a hostage whilst Kovpak's signallers radioed Moscow to confirm his identity. Whilst waiting for a reply, Chorny was introduced to Kovpak who said, 'Lay your gun down', to which Chorny replied, 'No I won't, you didn't give it to me.' When the CHQPM confirmed Chorny as one of Medvedev's fighters the situation lightened.

Kovpak commanded one of the few significant groups of partisans from Ukraine. He had fought the German occupation forces in 1918 and then been a member of the Soviet partisan forces during the Russian Civil War. From September 1941, as Chairman of the Sumy-Putivl *Oblast* in Ukraine he had organised a large and efficient partisan group. Under orders from Stalin himself Kovpak's force was to carry out a long-range penetration that aimed to reach the Carpathian Mountains. A lack of information regarding the precise nature of this expedition has led to considerable speculation and, almost all, the conclusions have a degree of validity. Certainly, such a long march through enemy territory would reinforce the likelihood of a return of Soviet power. Furthermore, any sabotage would be useful, as would sowing doubt in the minds of collaborators. Even more useful would be the destruction of the Galician oil fields. A German report speculated that its purpose may have been to link up with Tito's forces. Indeed, under interrogation, captured partisans nominated both Hungary and Romania as destinations.

There was also the possibility that Slovakia, where Hitler's puppet regime was facing increased opposition, was a probable target.

Having left their winter quarters in the Bryansk area and contacted Medvedev, sections of his group guided Kovpak's force by safe routes to Dubno. Chorny remembered one of Kovpak's men describing the Winners disparagingly, 'you aren't a partisan platoon but a school for noble girls'. Chorny, tactfully, did not reply but remarked to his colleagues that, 'in Kovpak's unit there was weaker discipline'. Putting aside such inter-formation rivalry, Kovpak's force was heavily equipped and organised along military lines. Its order of battle consisted of 5 infantry battalions of roughly 600 men each with 20 light and heavy machine guns and as many as 15 demolition experts and engineers. The artillery unit deployed 4 76mm guns, at least 5 45mm anti-tank guns and an anti-aircraft section with 20mm pieces that could be deployed against ground targets. A mounted scout platoon of 120 troopers was responsible for screening this body, as well as providing cover for the transport. One source quotes the latter as having up to 300 motor vehicles, which seems rather strange as this is not mentioned elsewhere. Generally, transport for such formations was the ubiquitous *panje* wagon. A large amount of ammunition and other supplies were carried. To keep supplies topped up the Red Air Force was to fly in to partisan-prepared airstrips. Communications were in the hands of a regular army officer and his two daughters. Incredible as it may seem, the Axis security forces appear to have been unaware of this large body of partisans and their wagon train for several months. Whether this was due to their focus being further to the east, where following the surrender of Sixth Army at Stalingrad there had been heavy fighting to restore the front, is anyone's guess. Continual movement, mainly at night, and the adroit use of camouflage were key elements in Kovpak's successful march westwards.

As news of his men's activities spread the Germans placed a reward on Kovpak's head, which almost overnight transformed him into a romantic, Robin Hood-like character. The plan to capture Kovpak was known as Operation Werewolf and involved a wide variety of security units. From June until early 1943 the Germans chased shadows. However, on 7 July the raiders were spotted from the air some 30km south-east of Tarnopol. Orders were issued to form a large net in to which the partisans were to be funnelled. When this was breached in mid-July the Luftwaffe committed more aircraft, including the specialist ground-attack machine, the HS129.

An airstrike resulted in the loss of 150 horses and combined with a growing number of casualties severely impaired the mobility of Kovpak's force. On 17 July the partisans were forced to abandon the bulk of their artillery. By now almost 2,000 German and an unknown number of Hungarian, Italian and Schuma units were involved in trying to bag Kovpak's force. But late, in a complete change of style, the partisans counter-attacked, resulting in them, once again, escaping the net. In late July Kovpak left the unit for Moscow, apparently placing it under the command of Major General S. V. Rudnev, the unit's political commissar, who was killed on 4 August and succeeded by Colonel P. P. Vershigora. From incomplete German reports it would seem that on 4 August there was a major engagement resulting in the death of Rudnev and 641 other 'bandits', with 100 prisoners taken. After the war Bach-Zelewski summed up Kovpak's men as 'the most fanatical and courageous partisans that I had ever seen'. High praise indeed.

Details of the unit's movements from that time until later in the year are vague. It seems to have continued to cause problems for the occupation forces but on a much-reduced scale. The operation became known as the Carpathian Raid.

However, during the time that Kovpak and Medvedev's forces were operating in north-western Ukraine the Axis had stepped up its security arrangements significantly.

A group of partisans, possibly the 'Winners', stand by the remains of a supply train. They are wearing what appear to be paratrooper jump suits. NKVD and army partisan formations wore as much uniform clothing as they could to help distinguish themselves from the civilian population; it was also a matter of pride in their appearance.

Nevertheless, when necessary they would don German or Schuma battalion clothing. The latter was worn when entering a village suspected of collaboration to flush out 'Fascist sympathisers' or to travel through Axis-dominated areas without raising too much suspicion.

A Soviet partisan disguised as a German officer. The uniform of is of a higher rank than that worn by Kuznetsov, and it does not display the Iron Cross ribbon he wore. The original caption implies, however, that it is Kuznetsov. Born in Siberia in 1911, he spoke fluent German having grown up in an area of German settlers. Furthermore, he was 'blonde and handsome and could pass as half German'. He was intercepted by Ukrainian nationalists in 1944 and died during the fire fight. Kuznetsov was created a posthumous Hero of the Soviet Union.

Gathering food was one of Boris Chorny's jobs. He paid the locals for food with Reichmarks. He was often asked, 'Why do you pay us German money?' 'Because you can use it,' was his reply. German requisitioned food warehouses were another source of supplies.

A working party of Russian POWs is escorted back through dense forest along a corduroy road. With a small escort, such as the one man seen here, such groups were easy prey for partisans, who often exploited such situations.

Agriculture was not the only industry exploited by the Germans. Here a German supervises textile production. Such factories produced uniforms for the Schuma and other locally raised formations. Very little found its way into the hands of the population, who were expected to make do and mend or go to the black market.

In Belorussia half-hearted attempts were made to invoke nationalist sentiment. However, such feelings were not deeply held by the ordinary people. Nevertheless, a youth organisation, loosely based on the Hitler Youth, was formed and members of it are possibly seen here.

From early 1942 onwards the occupied territories were 'harvested' for labour to work on farms and in factories in the Reich. Initially, volunteers were called for but as news of the conditions they lived in filtered back to their families, the volunteer system was soon replaced by simple round-ups. Several million Soviet citizens were thus shipped off only to face suspicion of collaboration for decades after.

In some Wehrmacht and Ostministerium circles moves had been afoot to raise Russian units to fight the Red Army proper, as there was a growing belief that 'only a Russian could beat a Russian'. One such was the ROA, the acronym for the Russian Army of Liberation, two officers of which are seen here attending a conference in Smolensk in 1943. Hitler barely tolerated the ROA and did not wish such organisations developed further.

German Army officers raised, almost as private initiatives, Ost Battalions which existed alongside more formal, ethnically acceptable formations, such as the Cossacks, for security tasks. One such is seen here preparing for an anti-partisan sweep in 1943. A mixed bag of uniform is apparent, both Soviet and obsolete German. Some were reliable, whilst others simply deserted to the partisans or melted into the forests to fend for themselves, fighting any who crossed their path.

By the second winter of the Russian campaign the Germans were better equipped and acclimatised to undertake winter warfare. Here skiers, of a police battalion, dressed in camouflage kit prepare for an anti-bandit sweep. Local children watch them leave a village.

A remarkable image of Kovpak, centre left with beard and black hat, dining with the family of a priest near Rovno in 1943. At odds with the popular perception of partisan life, it shows that such 'normal' events were still possible behind enemy lines. Vershigora, one of Kovpak's staff, took a series of photographs during the Carpathian Raid. It is possible that this is one of those.

D. S. Korotchenko, a powerful member of the Ukrainian Communist Party, is seen here with a group of Komsomol (Communist youth organisation) and Party workers in the enemy's rear during the early summer of 1943. As well as meeting partisan commanders and political officers, he found time to distribute medals. Kovpak can be seen in the centre. Unfortunately, the young medal recipient's name is lost. Such eminent visitors did much to boost the Party's image in the occupied regions.

Generally, life was more mundane, food preparation for such a large body of partisans as that under Kovpak's command was a serious undertaking. The woman stirs whilst the man butchers. To the rear is what appears to be a line of washing.

Dress regulations for this member of Kovpak's force seem to have been interpreted rather loosely. The hooded rain cape that doubled as a shelter portion is standard issue, in khaki, as are the trousers. The shirt and hat add a somewhat rakish look. However, the PPSh41 sub-machine gun, without its drum magazine here, was a simple but deadly weapon with a high rate of fire, thus ideally suited for the terrain.

What appears to be one of Kovpak's machine-gun sections is put through its paces. The most numerous machine here is the 7.62mm DP Model 1928 with its distinctive flat-pan magazine, which gave rise to the nickname of 'record player'. The shouldered machine gun appears to be a German MG34. Such captured weapons were often used, although they proved difficult to maintain due to their highly engineered build. Further down the line, near the drill master, is an anti-tank rifle often used by snipers or against soft-skinned vehicles.

Part of the artillery that accompanied Kovpak is seen here fording a stream. The gun is a 76mm Model 1927 infantry close-support piece. Designed to be light and easily manoeuvred by only a couple of men or animals, it was, again, simple to maintain and operate. Its short barrel meant that it was easy to use in thick undergrowth. The gun shield seems to have been dispensed with.

Two very worried German prisoners taken by Kovpak's unit during the Carpathian Raid sit waiting to hear their fate. Their tunics have been removed for partisans to use as disguises. Tales of what the partisans did to POWs were the stuff of nightmares for Axis security and policemen, as the discovery of their mutilated corpses was not unknown.

The slow progress of Kovpak's raid was, in part, due to the fact that considerable time was taken up locating and making camp. It was acknowledged by the Germans that the Soviets were masters of camouflage. Here one of Kovpak's anti-tank guns is under the beginnings of its cover. It is a 45mm Model 1937 gun that has had its wheels changed. The guard is wearing his medal, as was traditional in the Russian armed forces even in the field.

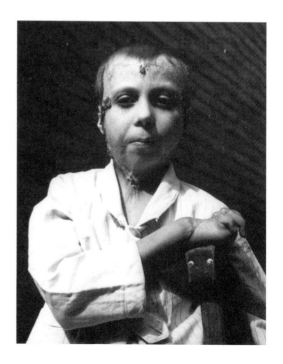

Whatever slogan or principle the partisans fought for, be it Communism, patriotism or simply to defeat an invader, there was always revenge hot or cold to be dealt out on behalf of those too young, old or infirm to do so themselves. This young Ukrainian girl has been tortured by the occupation forces. A heated band was placed around her head that contracted as it cooled. Other injuries, to her hands and legs (hence the crutch), were also inflicted. The offence was unrecorded in the original caption. News of such events often travelled further than it was meant to.

Chapter Seven

Bandenbekampfung – Bandit Warfare

The summer of 1942 proved to be the high point of Axis expansion into the USSR. By then 45 per cent of the pre-war population zone, 33 per cent of the industrial capacity and almost 50 per cent of its agricultural land was occupied. Soviet attempts to mobilise the people of the 'Temporarily Occupied Lands' had been stepped up and their numbers increased: although Stalin's pronouncement on May Day that 'The Soviet areas occupied by the Germans are swept by the flames of partisan warfare' was something of an exaggeration. Nevertheless, the Germans sought to improve their counter-measures. In part, this would be achieved in terms of psychology and perception. Himmler had begun to insist on substituting the word 'bandit' for that of partisan in SS and police reports and documents. From now on partisan hunts and sweeps would become bandit hunts. No longer were the partisans to be viewed as anything more than 'gangsters' or 'highwaymen', who 'then flee, hoping to encumber the innocent inhabitants [who] will be held responsible for their deeds'. To support this concept a leafleting campaign was begun in towns and villages across the occupied territories. This move by Himmler was given Hitler's backing in Directive 46, issued on 18 August 1942. However, as a Directive and not a direct Führer Order it was open to flexibility of interpretation, depending on local circumstances and the local security and political authorities.

Directive 46 emphasised army–SS co-operation. The army was to clear bandits from the operational zone, which extended for 40km behind the front line. In that area the SS and the police would carry out ethnic cleansing. Six points covered the priorities:

All staffs regardless of the parent organisation or branch of service were expected to engage in *Bandenbekampfung*.

Operations were to be active – the war was to be taken to the partisans, simple passive activities, such a guarding a facility, were no longer acceptable.

Efforts should be made to regain civilian confidence by behaving justly.

Sufficient food should be left to civilians to ensure a minimum level of sustenance.
Unspecified rewards for collaborators were to be allowed but bandit
   sympathisers were to be dealt with mercilessly.
 Finally, the troops were warned not to be over-trusting of the locals, particularly
   those in Axis employ.

Manpower was to be increased, not by recruiting more locals but by re-deploying units of the army's reserve and training units from Germany and elsewhere in Europe. Administratively, the Government General of Poland, which included Galicia and the territory around Lvov, became a Home Forces district and gained two army divisions. Five reserve divisions were allocated to Ukraine and the Baltic States and a further 50,000 reserves would be moved into other parts of the rear behind the Eastern Front. Additionally, RAD units, railway security troops, foresters and agricultural and economic management groups would also be armed and expected to fight the bandits. The relocation of forces was to be carried out before November 1942. As Hitler said, 'Victory will go to the strong ... at all costs we will establish law and order there'.

Two supplements were added to Directive 46. The so-called 'Commando Order', aimed at curbing the activities of British and American Special Forces, which stated such troops were 'to be slaughtered' and that such executions were to be recorded, noting 'a sabotage, terror or destruction unit has been encountered and exterminated to the last man'. Directive 46 was to apply wherever the German security writ ran.

Himmler appointed, temporarily, as his Inspector for Bandit Warfare across the Eastern Front SS *Obergruppenfuhrer* (General) Erich von dem Bach-Zelewski, a man of considerable experience from his post of HSSPF behind AGC. A similar post was created by Schenkendorff for the army, Major General Walter Warlimont.

The main thrust of Directive 46 was to extend German control over the occupied territories and into the countryside where the partisans had enjoyed considerable freedom of movement. The SS issued guidelines on methods that it hoped would prove fruitful in curbing this situation. Bandit hunts were to be carried out quickly, utilising surprise and with a minimum of 'spilling German blood'. Executions, 'of bandit suspects', were to be carried out quietly to avoid 'inflaming the natives'.

Bach-Zelewski passed his probationary period and was confirmed as Plenipotentiary for Bandenbekampfung in the East on 23 October 1942. Having met with his army opposite number, he turned his attention to liquidating the 'bandits, Jews and bandit suspects' in the Pripet Marshes. This measure was designed to prevent them from preparing their winter quarters. The operation was code named

Hamburg. Schuma battalions, stiffened by 1st SS Infantry Brigade and the notorious SS *Sonnder Kommando* Dirlewanger, carried out a series of sweeps against various partisan groups.

As the concluding report pointed out, 'the territory was re-opened for the German administration after it had been ruled by bandits for months'. The coldly specific body count listed, '1,674 bandits killed in action', 1,510 suspects (unspecified) as well as, '2,988 bandit sympathisers' executed and 2,958 Jews killed.

Nor had the army been inactive, with reports concluding favourably on the successful application of Directive 46. During November 1942 the army issued instructions that lauded 'honourable treatment for bandit deserters', but also the killing of those bandits who resisted and severe punishment for population centres found to have supported them. Such punishments ranged from food confiscation to total destruction. Satisfied with progress, Hitler issued, via Field Marshal Keitel, a final order relating to bandit fighting. Noting that some officers had been accused of misconduct during bandit sweeps, this state of affairs would no longer be the case. Bandit warfare in the east was to undertaken without fear because, 'no German employed in Bandenbekampfung . . . can be made responsible for their actions before the courts'. Success was now all that counted and this was usually measured by the body count.

However, success at the front was an experience being savoured by the Red Army. At Stalingrad Hitler's largest formation, Sixth Army, was dying by inches in a shattered wasteland of burned out factories and derelict homes. Sixth Army's surrender on 2 February 1943 marked the beginning of the retreat that would end in Berlin just over two years later. As in previous winters, Soviet offensive security troops, though a smaller percentage, were drawn into the front line with the effect that operations were scaled down at a time when the partisans were at their most vulnerable due to the lack of cover, heat and supplies.

Nevertheless, anti-partisan sweeps continued. Operation Hornung, again in the Pripet Marshes, yielded, between 8 and 26 February, '2,219 dead bandits, 7,378 persons who received special treatment, 65 prisoners, 3,300 Jews'. Special treatment was a phrase open to interpretation as it could include deportation to the Reich as slave labourers or death. Deportees could have been the registered inhabitants of a village that it was deemed necessary to destroy. Jews were automatically murdered. This was particularly tragic for, as Boris Chorny, himself a Jew, remembered, 'Jewish people were fed by us [Medvedev's partisan unit].' However, as Medvedev [half Jewish] told Chorny, 'we can't feed them all . . . we'll give them one or two rifles and send them to Belorussia', where it was believed to be easier for them to survive. Chorny was asked to accompany them part of the way, but the group gradually dispersed. Returning to his unit Chorny was told by Medvedev, 'don't worry we gave them a chance, we aren't here to guard them'. Albert Tsessarsky recalled some Jews were 'admitted to our group and fought well'. Jewish partisan units were formed by escapees from the numerous ghettoes and camps in the occupied territories of the east. As the local Jewish population was exterminated, so more arrived from elsewhere in Europe to work and await their turn to die. Those lucky enough to escape from Nazi persecution often found themselves exposed to the anti-Semitism of local people. Even if they were not turned over to the authorities, they were either robbed or simply told to move on. The most famous Jewish partisan formation was that recruited by the Bielski brothers which took in refugees of all ages, backgrounds and genders. For the majority of partisan units, however, the brutal reality of survival, combat and nomadic movement was sufficient without the added responsibility of refugees, often from the towns, who were ill-prepared for the rigours of life in the semi-wilderness where they operated.

Following the defeat at Stalingrad and the subsequent advance of the Red Army large swathes of eastern Ukraine were liberated, as was the Caucasus other than the Taman Peninsula close by Crimea. The Germans finally stabilised the front along a line east of Smolensk, Orel and Kharkov down to the Sea of Azov near Mariupol. North of Orel up to the siege lines around Leningrad little had changed.

News of the Axis' disaster spread throughout the occupied territories like wildfire. Partisan presses and the propagandists at the CHQPM produced millions of leaflets and news sheets describing the kilometres of cold, sickly, malnourished Axis POWs wending their way eastwards. Naturally, this news led many collaborators and native members of the security forces to consider their futures, which certainly appeared to be darker than twelve months before, as indeed did that of the Axis.

A pause in the Axis advance across the open steppes towards the Volga River. Sleeping on the bonnet of their Sd.Kfz 250, these German soldiers have no concerns about snipers or partisan activity.

Despite the speed of Army Group South's advance, prisoners were considerably fewer in number than during the summer of 1941. It is clear from this image how open the terrain in the eastern Ukraine was.

As the advance continued, the demand for supplies routed through the rear of AGC increased. This 20mm anti-aircraft gun is positioned so that it can fire at ground as well as aerial targets. Troop transports such as this were rarely attacked.

A market stall in a town behind German lines carries on with business under a sign for the local Field Police.

'The German command will reward those who capture the bandit "Katya" with 3,000 Marks, 5 pouds [82kg] of salt and a 25 hectare plot of land.' Clearly, this was an important young lady to merit such a bounty on her head.

And the Soviet riposte, in Belorussian, 'Death to the German Occupiers'. It continues, 'Down with the Hitlerite German imperialist gangsters who broke the peace between the peoples and threw Germany, Europe and the USSR into the turmoil of war!'

Germany's contradictory and confusing land-reform policies were brushed under the carpet for this propaganda image. A Ukrainian farmer discusses his collective farm's output statistics for 1943 with Reich agricultural officials. There are '409 workers' farming a total arable area of 735 hectares along with 112 hectares of pasture. By this time few if any believed any change would come.

Surrounding their commander and commissar, a large partisan group prepares for a mission. The man to the right front is carrying a field-modified German rifle with a magazine designed for a Soviet automatic rifle. The variety of small arms could create logistical nightmares for the supply officers.

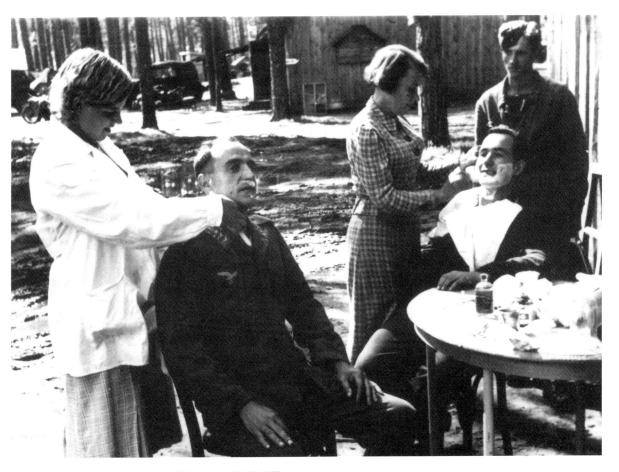

On 22 September 1943 Reichskommisar Ostland Wilhelm Kube was assassinated in his official residence in Minsk by one of his maids, Yelena Mazanik, who escaped to join the local partisans. Trust in local workers, such as these seen here, was often misplaced.

The entrance to a partisan bunker, well camouflaged and probably with an equally well-hidden rear exit.

A German lookout post built on top of a church to take advantage of the view.

Three Focke-Wulf 189s, such as this one, were assigned to reconnaissance and bombing missions in support of anti-bandit operations. It was capable of carrying 200kg of bombs and had extremely good all-round vision due to its extensively glazed fuselage area.

Partisans in the Caucasus. When Colonel Kocharov, leader of the Karachai Red Partisan group, escaped from German captivity he was executed as a member of a 'traitor nation' due to the welcome the Karachai, a Caucasian people, gave to the Germans in 1942. The majority of the Karachai people were deported to Kazakhstan in late 1943 by the NKVD for collaboration.

Kalmyk partisans in early 1943. Although many of their race were staunchly anti-Soviet, there were a good number who fought in the partisans and the Red Army. When their homeland, near Stalingrad, was cleared of Axis forces the Buddhist Kalmyks were deported en masse.

Death to the German Occupiers', both a slogan and the name of a partisan unit.

German police ford a stream in Belarus, hauling their cart of equipment behind them.

A German base camp for a Jagd Kommando formation, the specialist 'bandit hunters' who ventured into the swamps and forests of the USSR in pursuit of the partisans. There were few such specialist troops as the need for them was not regarded as important until it was too late.

A Belarussian veteran of the First World War, the Russian Civil War and now the partisan war.

The banner of the All Union Leninist Communist Youth League Central Committee (Komsomol). It belongs to the Komsomol organisation in a partisan detachment.

And the work of the partisans continues.

Chapter Eight

Rail War and Concert

By the spring of 1943 the overhauls and organisational changes regarding partisan/bandit warfare carried out by the Soviets and the Germans were well under way. But it was the front line that was uppermost in the minds of Hitler and Stalin. As the muddy season drew to a close and the ground became solid, plans were laid for the summer campaigning season.

Amongst the intelligence gathered by Kuznetsov was information about the German plans for an offensive. When collated with other such reports the German plans became clearer. The fighting of February–March had left the Red Army holding a rectangular bulge around the city of Kursk, an important road and rail hub. The Kursk salient had the potential to act as a springboard for any Soviet offensive to threaten AGC or AGS or indeed both. It also looked an inviting target on the maps. Lacking the resources for a large operation on a par with the previous summer, Hitler viewed the salient as a realistically obtainable objective. The German plan called for simultaneous attacks into the northern and southern corners of the salient from Orel and Belgorod respectively. Soviet planning was simple; defend the salient in massive depth and, assuming a successful defence, a series of counter-offensives aimed at both AGC and AGS.

The partisan contribution was to increase their attacks on German road and rail transport networks, particularly the railways as it was by this means that the large numbers of tanks would be moved up to the front, as well as the millions of litres of fuel and mountains of munitions that would be required. During the winter of 1942–1943 attacks on the rail system behind AGC had increased considerably in an effort to disrupt support for the Stalingrad relief operation and the subsequent efforts to stabilise the front around Kharkov. The most serious dislocation of this traffic occurred when the railway bridge over the Desna River, 20km south-west of Briansk, was overrun by partisans. Smaller scale acts took place at many other points, increasing in frequency from 626 in April to 841 in June in AGC's rear alone. Naturally, this increase in activity triggered a response from the security forces. Of all the anti-bandit expeditions carried out at this time Operation Cottbus, named after a city in Brandenburg, in the rear of AGC was particularly significant. Involving the SS, including the police, the army and the Luftwaffe, planning had been underway from early May and was directed at the large partisan formations in the quadrilateral formed by Polotsk, Vitebsk, Orsha and Borisov. The quadrilateral enclosed some 2,750sq km centred on Lepel, which lay roughly 150km west of Smolensk. The region contained over 10,000 partisans and was bounded by important rail lines on all sides.

The terrain was mainly dense woodland that thinned out towards the south between Borisov and Orsha. As the German order noted, 'Because of the still unclear enemy situation and because of the terrain a very active and extensive close reconnaissance of the paths has to be carried out.' Elsewhere, the same order required, 'It is proven that Bandits posing as harmless farmers are trying to escape this must be stopped under all circumstances. Retreating bands, after our experience, use hidden paths that are partly covered by water into the swamp areas . . . these . . . areas must be penetrated and combed out.' Tactically, Cottbus would be an encirclement.

From 3–28 June Operation Cottbus ran its dreadful course. Of the 8,700 men committed just over half were German. The bulk of the fighting was undertaken by Belorussian and Ukrainian Schuma battalions. From Dirlewanger's unit of poachers, murderers and other assorted criminals 3,500 also participated. The Russian collaborationist 1st National SS Brigade contributed 2,500 men who were expected to infiltrate the partisan camps and attack from within. Apparently, this part of the operation failed and the Russian SS men took heavy casualties. They worked off their consequent frustration by slaughtering civilians by the hundred; an activity paralleled by Dirlewanger's thugs.

The initial post-operation report listed an incredible haul of booty including an aircraft, a dozen gliders, 10 large field guns, 19 anti-tank guns but a mere 905 rifles. The latter contrasted with the body count of 6,000 partisans killed in action and 4,000 bandit sympathisers executed. A total of 2,400 civilians were rounded up for forced labour and 600 prisoners were taken. Specifically, German casualties were 127 dead and over 500 wounded, which, when compared with similar operations, was very high. Figures for the number of Jewish dead are unavailable.

As Operation Cottbus wound down the CHQPM had begun to plan for its most ambitious offensive to date, Operation Rail War, which was the work of two former destruction battalion commanders. It was to begin on 3 August with the aim of disrupting the railways behind all three German army groups but particularly AGC. Stavka assumed a successful defence of the Kursk salient that would be followed by a series of Soviet offensives rippling to left and right of Kursk.

By mid-July Operation Citadel was all but over. As the Red Air Force flew tons of explosives and dozens of engineers in to the waiting partisans, plans were finalised for Rail War.

The CHQPM had issued orders to its regional staffs which had been passed down the chains of command. A total of 167 units, optimistically numbering over 100,000 partisans, then made their own plans. On 13 July Hitler called off Operation Citadel and within days the Soviet counter-offensives began. The night of 2–3 August marked the start of Operation Rail War. It would appear from partisan unit reports that during the first night 42,000 individual rails were damaged either by explosives or simply torn up. Particular groups were allocated to destroy specific lengths of track but it was not only the rails that were targeted. AGC's transport report for August noted, 'Another major handicap . . . was the increasing number of sabotage acts, committed chiefly by native workers under partisan orders. These acts resulted chiefly in a severe shortage of locomotives.' Acts such as putting explosives in coal bunkers, holing pipes in the engines, draining brake fluid and loosening bolts all contributed to the overall aim as much as high explosives. The report continued, 'the daily average amounted to 45 demolitions . . . 20,000 demolition charges went off . . . 4,528 mines were removed. Within two nights 9,600km–11,000kms of track in the area were cut in 8,422 places . . . several lines could not be put back into operation for a considerable time'.

Unit commanders who did not appear to be as active as the CHQPM required were threatened with disciplinary action. Indeed, post-war Soviet studies were critical of the partisans behind AGS and AGN who appear to have achieved little in comparison with those behind AGC. The degree to which Operation Rail War caused problems for the Germans will doubtless remain a cause for debate for decades. However, it is an indisputable fact that the German defeat at Kursk and the retreat of both AGS and AGN lead to an upsurge in partisan recruitment and desertion from the locally raised security units.

An AGC report commented,

In many instances, the so-called Eastern Volunteer units, employed to protect the railways, made common cause with the partisans . . . An entire Russian security detachment, 600 men, went over to the partisans. On 17 August [it] attacked Krulevskchizna railway station. Using machine guns, mortars, anti-tank guns [they] caused considerable damage. German losses in that engagement 240 dead, 491 wounded.

The defeats at Stalingrad and then Kursk confirmed in the minds of those in the occupied territories that Germany's ultimate defeat was, if not imminent, then very much more likely than its ultimate victory. This new wave of recruits led to an interesting development within partisan formations. The longer established members viewed the newcomers as 'bandwagon jumpers', only prepared to commit themselves when victory was apparently a given. The influx of recruits led to many units detaching platoons or companies to form the nuclei of new units. An example of this is the Kirovskaya Brigade in Belarus which detached a company that grew into the Ordzhonikidze formation, which, during the summer of 1943, had the following generally accepted structure: a commander, a commissar, a chief of staff, a deputy commander for reconnaissance, a deputy commissar for youth activities and deputy chiefs of staff responsible for supplies and healthcare.

As these new recruits and more formal organisational styles were being absorbed, the time was growing close for the commencement of the second phase of Operation Rail War. Operation Concert was scheduled to begin on 19 September, but due to the poor weather the supply air bridge broke down, resulting in a lack of explosives. It was postponed for a week. Another rash of demolitions was to break out across the rears of all three army groups, but the entire number of rails disabled was only 150,000. Although a significant number, the repairs were effected rapidly and movement was not interrupted to the same extent as during the summer. Red Army leaders, such as Zhukov and Rokossovsky, were fulsome in their praise of the partisans' contribution to the regular forces' success during the second half of 1943. Both were writing with a considerable degree of political correctness, and the magnanimity of the professional, but the partisans did make a contribution to that year's advances if only by depriving the Germans of their full confidence in and use of their supply lines. Nor had there been any let up in anti-partisan activities during the summer, and by autumn this had become an almost a continual drain on manpower and resources.

As AGS fell back first to the Dnieper River and then into western Ukraine, AGC withdrew to a line 75km west of Smolensk and roughly 175km west of Bryansk, thus forming the so-called Belorussian Balcony. In AGS's wake streamed a host of refugees, thousands of known collaborators, informers, members of the security forces, even those who had expressed negative thoughts about Stalin and the Soviet system that were more than locally acceptable. Only the position of AGN had changed but little during 1943 but it was to be the first area in which the partisans would make their first important effort during the winter of 1943–1944.

The legacy of Stalingrad. Axis corpses wait for interment in a mass grave on the outskirts of the city.

Preparations for Operation Citadel, the German summer offensive, continued apace. Here men of SS Panzer Grenadier Division Das Reich are transported by rail to their assembly point.

Soviet infantry prepare mortar positions. Thousands of kilometres of trenches and hundreds of gun positions were dug inside the salient.

'Wet Triangle' was a security operation carried out along the Desna River near Kiev during May 1943. The German Water Police were called on to supply fire support with three vessels such as this.

By late 1942 nearly all the mines laid by the partisans were wooden and thus undetectable by minesweeping equipment.

Rebuilding the railway bridge over the Desna River to the point where it was capable of supporting trains of wagons without their locomotive took little more than a week of prodigious effort. It was one of the most disruptive partisan acts of 1943.

S. E. Pisarevich, a member of the 'Partisan Brigade Buddeny'. This formation fought in the Pinsk region. A unit in this area, 'destroyed four railway bridges, three water pump houses . . . and burned down a railway sleeper production plant', as described in an AGC report.

River transport was also a target. One of the few successes accorded to the Ukrainian partisans was the sinking of the German patrol boat *Leipzig*, seen here after it had been run aground. A total of eighty-nine other vessels of all types were sunk by Ukrainian units.

SS troops leave a burning village during the anti-bandit Operation Cormorant during May 1943.

For the German troops involved in forming the security cordon the waiting was often the hardest part. Sitting under their makeshift shelter, a group of Germans play cards to pass the time.

Moving during the hours of daylight could be problematic if the Luftwaffe was involved. Again, with the density of ground cover it was an easy matter for the partisans to conceal themselves.

Preparing a demolition charge during Operation Rail War. As well as demolition equipment, the CHQPM supplied, during the second half of 1943, over 700 mortars, 17,000 machine guns and 200,000 hand grenades to partisan groups under its control.

As well as patrolling the lines with armoured trains, the German security forces employed captured tanks, such as these French Somua S-35s, in a pursuit role. The side panels of the wagon would drop to allow the tank to drive off after the partisans.

However, the results were not always positive for the Germans. The partisans would lure tanks into mined areas or use anti-tank guns on them. The Somua had a crew of three with the commander acting as gunner, loader and aimer and consequently the reaction time was slow with sometimes fatal consequences. The Somua was replaced with the more useful Skoda-built Panzer 38(t).

Although very difficult to interpret, the original caption for this image declares it to be one of the 'Gas Trucks' used by the Einsatzgruppen. Their victims were sealed into the rear and poisoned by the re-directed exhaust fumes as the lorry drove around. This vehicle was destroyed by partisans in Crimea.

A particularly successful attack on a German supply train.

As part of their hearts and minds effort, partisan units organised social, cultural and educational events within their districts. Clearly, one such event is in progress here.

Another poster in Belorussian but written on birch bark. It reads, 'Death to the German Occupants! Long live the 26th anniversary of the Great October Revolution! All our forces for the support or our heroic Red Army and our glorious Red Navy! All forces of the people – for the demolition of the enemy! Forward, to our victory! (Stalin)'.

As the Germans withdrew across Ukraine, they destroyed the very infrastructure they had previously fought to defend. The hook at the rear of this locomotive will be dropped between the tracks and then plough up the sleepers as it is driven away.

Each partisan unit had a reconnaissance platoon. One of the most important tasks they carried out was the capture of 'tongues', POWs for interrogation. This interestingly posed image purports to show a German 'tongue' being questioned during the summer of 1943. His Iron Cross is in an interesting position.

Chapter Nine

Bagration, Belarus and Beyond

Often overlooked, due to the scale of partisan operations behind AGC, the partisan formations to the rear of AGN were to take centre stage as 1944 dawned. During 1942 there had been little activity in the north but the Leningrad Partisan HQ had worked hard to increase the number and efficiency of the units it oversaw. Consolidation of small bands into larger ones and a ruthless review of the qualities of the leaders resulted, by the summer of 1943, in a considerably more effective force. As the area under the control of the LPHQ was smaller than that of, for example, Belarus communications, control and co-ordination were simpler. By the end of 1943 10 partisan brigades, numbering '35,000 active fighters and thousands of auxiliaries' were in place. During October 1943 Fifth Partisan Brigade captured the town of Plijusa on the Luga–Pskov rail line to prevent the deportation of the civilian population. This action was replicated by other formations across the rear of AGN. Indeed, it was the groundswell of popular disaffection that was to lead to Hitler's decision to withdraw to the Panther Line when the Red Army offensive was gaining momentum four months later.

The Soviets intended to drive AGN away from the Leningrad district into the Baltic States and began their attack on 14 January 1944. Partisan attacks did not begin until virtually all the security troops had been committed to the front line. It was on the evening of 16 January that the partisans began to interfere with the railways by destroying Tolmachevo station. The following night a more general series of attacks on security posts and the track itself were carried out. By 20 January the railway situation was described as 'tense' and in some areas as 'completely paralysed'. Supply and troop transports ground to a halt as partisan attacks increased 'tremendously'. The 8th Jaeger Division took four days to move and then only partially into position, three days later than anticipated due to the mining of both road and railway. As the Germans withdrew, NKVD personnel were parachuted into Estonia and Latvia to organise partisan groups. By mid-February the Eighth Leningrad Partisan Brigade was identified heading for Latvia. Active measures by the

HSSPF Ostland had drafted thousands of Estonian, Latvian and Lithuanian Schuma troops to deal with this threat – they succeeded, intercepting the partisans in a series of running fights. The majority of the partisans from the Leningrad region had been enrolled in the Red Army but the surviving infiltrators behind AGN confined their activities to propaganda and intelligence work due to the general antipathy of the locals to the prospect of Soviet liberation.

Far to the south in Ukraine Medvedev and Kovpak's units still continued their combat and propaganda missions. The Chief of Staff of the Ukrainian Partisan Movement, Colonel General Strokach, was, by late 1943, closely connected with the regular army and expanding his role to look beyond the borders of the USSR. Rather than just sending partisan units behind Axis lines, where the fighting with nationalists was increasing and with much of Ukraine back under Soviet control, Strokach's staff began to train pro-Soviet partisans for operations in Poland and Czechoslovakia. Whatever motives were announced for these activities during the winter of 1943–1944, the long-term aim was to lay the foundations for future Communist regimes in those countries. Czechoslovakia, of which only Slovakia nominally existed, and Poland both had governments in exile in Britain, of which Stalin fundamentally disapproved. However, both had partisan movements and those of Poland were mainly anti-Soviet. The Polish Home Army (the AK) was a large, active and well-organised force that operated in both German and Soviet-claimed Poland. The AK wanted a return to Poland's pre-1939 frontiers which effectively put it at odds with the USSR's claims to western Ukraine and Belarus. The Ukrainian Partisan Staff was, therefore, to bend its efforts to create a pro-Soviet, Communist partisan force to match the AK in those areas. By January 1944 the Red Army had crossed into pre-war Polish territory into land Moscow coveted. The Polish government in exile had ordered the AK to support Soviet operations, but Polish partisans could not be mobilised into the Soviet-sponsored Polish Army. In western Ukraine and Galicia NKVD partisan units, such as those of Medvedev, and those organised by Strokach operated regardless of international boundaries. When a frontier was crossed the unit commander would open his sealed orders that generally read that he should 'act according to the existing conditions'. Fighting promptly broke out with the AK when the Soviets began to bring the tiny GL (Guardija Ludowa) into play. The GL was a Polish Communist Party partisan group. Members of the GL were flown to a Ukrainian Partisan Staff's training camp where they had prepared for operations in Poland. In April 1944 the Polish Staff for the Partisan Movement was set up in Rovno, overseen by Strokach, to control the GL units that were now operating against the Germans, the AK and the Ukrainian nationalists. At the same time the Czechoslovak Communist Party appealed to Moscow for help in waging a partisan war. Once again a training cadre was taken in by Strokach's staff. During the spring and summer of 1944 bases were established, particularly in Slovakia, and covert recruitment of local partisans began. Their situation was helped by the Red Air Force that flew in supplies almost at will due to the Luftwaffe's weakness over Eastern Europe.

Finally, on 28 August 1944 the Slovaks rose up against their pro-Nazi government, but the country was, during the course of the next week, overrun by a motley collection of German troops. A Soviet attempt to alleviate the situation, by elements of First Ukrainian Front battling its way through the Carpathian Mountains, failed. By the end of October the Slovakian Uprising was over, but, nevertheless, some stragglers fought on in the mountains. The Soviet effort in Slovakia was certainly greater than that made to support the Warsaw Uprising of August 1944. When that tragic event ended in the defeat of the AK there were many stragglers who made their way east. With the AK apparently a broken force, Stalin directed the NKVD to round-up any units found in Soviet territory. Interestingly, such partisans were referred to in NKVD reports as, 'illegal formations, rebels or bandits'. Indeed, round-ups of AK fighters had been going on for months prior to the Warsaw Uprising. One unit, answering the call to go to Warsaw in July to reinforce the forthcoming uprising, had arrived east of the city at the same time as the Red Army. Having liberated several villages in the wake of the retreating Germans, they suddenly radioed a message, un-coded, that was intercepted in Britain, 'they [Red Army] are approaching us . . . they are disarming us'. The foundations were being laid for the Soviet liberation of Poland.

For the Soviet partisans the stage for its most impressive operation had been set several months before. During the winter of 1943–1944 the Soviet fronts facing AGC had been relatively quiet. Hitler, convinced that the next series of Soviet offensives would continue to push against AGS, had split that front into two, Army Group South Ukraine (AGSU) and Army Group North Ukraine (AGNU). The latter was expected to be the target and, therefore, was the strongest in terms of armour. The southern flank of AGC ran south-west from Bobruisk just below the Pripet Marshes to a point west of Lutsk and the AGNU and AGSU took over with fronts that sloped eastwards to the Black Sea west of Odessa.

From the spring of 1944 onwards Moscow had received a stream of intelligence reports that detailed AGC's order of battle and defensive preparations. More and more partisan and NKVD intelligence-gathering operations were carried out. Before this the NKVD had tended to act alone due to a lack of trust in partisans other than their own units. The reason for this was simple: the NKVD was afraid of its agents falling into the hands of German-run 'mock partisan' bands who operated in the hope of flushing out the real thing and bandit sympathisers. However, the orders under which the partisans now operated did not come from the CHQPM, as that body had been wound up on 13 January 1944.

The responsibility for the partisans now rested with the Communist Party of the appropriate republic and its local regional hierarchy. The partisans were directed, by the Belorussian Communist Party's Central Committee, to cease operations behind AGC to encourage the Germans to reinforce their belief that the offensive was aimed at AGNU. Then, on 20 June, they unleashed another Operation Rail War. This time the targets were the one heavy capacity, double-tracked line and the five lower capacity lines on which AGC depended. The few-surviving German records are slim but indicate almost two-thirds of the 4,000 demolition attempts succeeded, 'the lines Minsk–Orsha and Mogilev–Vitebsk were especially hard hit and almost completely paralysed for several days'. The Soviets calculated that 'the partisan bands blew up 40,000 rails and derailed 147 trains'. Roads were mined and convoys attacked.

Operation Bagration burst across the lines of AGC in a series of waves from 22 June 1944, three years to the day after Operation Barbarossa had provoked the Great Patriotic War, as the Soviets termed it. However, as the Red Army advanced up to 50km per day, AGC began to collapse, the partisans came out into the open. Several units had been ordered to ambush and mount delaying attacks on retreating German forces and to try and secure river crossings. The latter efforts were generally unsuccessful but the former were not. As German units, escaping from cities such as Vitebsk, disintegrated under air and artillery fire, the partisans, eager for revenge, struck. With no facilities for and probably less inclination to take prisoners, the partisans, their numbers augmented by any civilians inclined to pick up a gun, wreaked a fearful toll. No figures are available but it is estimated that up to 20,000 German troops died trying to escape from the Vitebsk encirclement. Similar episodes occurred throughout Belarus during the last week of June and into July. Within a week the Red Army had reached and crossed the Berezina River and on 3 July entered Minsk, capital of Belarus. AGC had dissolved in less than a month.

Across Belarus thousands of partisans were drafted into the regular army, whilst others took the opportunity to go 'Fritz hunting' alongside special army units tasked with flushing out German stragglers, of which there were thousands wandering amidst the marshes and forests.

The partisan parade in Minsk effectively signalled the end of the 'amateur' partisan.

Now it was the time for the NKVD, the 'professionals', such as Vershigora's 1st Ukrainian Partisan Division, to head west to continue with their old and new tasks. A partisan medal, in two classes, was struck and issued liberally. In the Baltic States and Ukraine nationalist partisans fought on against Soviet rule for over a decade.

Simultaneously, the Soviet partisan movement rapidly became enshrined in many, somewhat embellished, official histories, films and other media forms.

Whilst there is no doubting the vileness of German rule in the occupied territories, there are grounds for doubting some of the tales of the partisans' achievements, but such histories are always written by the victors. Nevertheless, for the ordinary men and women who lived and fought against the invader it was a time in their lives of which they have every right to be justly proud. There is no doubt that they made a definite contribution to the victory over the Third Reich by their very defiance.

A member of a partisan group near Vilnius, capital of Lithuania. Support for the partisan movement was weak in the Baltic States. However, the United Partisan Organisation, an exclusively Jewish umbrella group, brought together Communists, Zionists and anti-Nazis of different beliefs. With the liquidation of the Vilnius ghetto in 1943, survivors, such as the lady seen here, escaped to join Soviet groups.

A collaborator is publicly executed by members of Fifth Leningrad Partisan Brigade in January 1944.

As elsewhere on the Eastern Front, the Germans found that the specialist equipment of the mountain troops was highly effective in bandit country. Here men of 5th Mountain Division prepare to fire their 75mm howitzer. Designed to be carried by six pack animals, it was an excellent weapon for use in such areas as this.

A typical German railway guard post on an isolated stretch of track. A perimeter of barbed wire encloses a more substantial wood and earth parapet. The undergrowth has been cleared for several hundred metres with off-cuts used to fill the ditch alongside the permanent way to prevent partisans using it as cover.

Kovpak's Carpathian expedition ended officially in October 1943, although his unit remained in the area. Kovpak, centre, is pictured here discussing the operation. To the left is N. S. Khrushchev, leader of the Ukrainian Communist Party, to the right, P. G. Tychyna, the Ukrainian Minister of Education and a famous poet.

A group of Polish partisans ride along on a Soviet T 20 Komsomolets artillery tractor. As the Red Army approached the Polish frontiers, the main Polish partisan movement, the AK, became increasingly concerned as to Soviet intentions. Clashes with Russian partisan groups became more frequent as the AK had been accused of, 'murdering communists'.

The Warsaw Uprising of August 1944 was carried out by the AK in an attempt to liberate their capital and pre-empt the arrival of the Red Army. Soviet efforts to assist the Poles, despite their proximity to the city and a call to arms on 29 July, were derisory. During the sixty-three days of fighting, beginning on 1 August, the city was destroyed and the AK crushed.

Army Group North Ukraine was expected to be the target of the Soviet summer offensive in 1944. To counter this threat the bulk of Germany's armour in the east was concentrated there. AGC was to base its defences on static lines and 'fortified' areas. As north–south railway communications were routed quite a way to the west, the time to reinforce either front would work to the Soviet's advantage.

During May 1944 the Crimean peninsula was cleared of Axis forces. Here a partisan group celebrates the liberation of Yalta.

During the spring of 1944 the Germans mounted several anti-bandit operations consecutively. The areas in which they were carried out were to the rear of Second, Third Panzer and Fourth armies which comprised much of AGC.

Watching and waiting along the perimeter of the encirclement during the anti-bandit operations of 1944.

Others watched and waited as well.

Security operations came to an end when Operation Bagration began. Amongst the tally of successes recorded were, '342 camps and 900 bunkers destroyed'. The remains of a camp are seen here.

Bandit hunters with an assortment of weapons, as befitted their second-line status. The machine gun appears to be a Czech-made ZB 30. Within days of Operation Bagration starting these troops were committed to front-line combat, for which they were totally unsuited.

'Fritz hunting' yields results during the summer of 1944.

Armed and dangerous still. Partisans exempted from conscription were drafted in to help gather the harvest. The formerly occupied territories were devastated and depopulated, therefore every effort was made to restore land to food production. Despite rigorous efforts, the USSR suffered from food shortages for several years following the end of the war.

German security men, administrators and those adjudged to be responsible for the atrocities carried out during the occupation were returned to the areas where they had committed their crimes for public execution.

In the wake of the Red Army came the NKVD to enquire into the activities of the locals during the years of occupation. Their judgements left no opportunity for appeal.

As Operation Bagration forged ahead, the arrival of partisan forces often presaged the official liberation.

Minsk race course witnessed the partisans' grand parade on 17 July 1944. As one participant recalled, 'They were met with enthusiasm, they marched proudly with medals on (their) chests! They were the winners!' Dozens of units were represented and hundreds of fighters marched past the podium where Ponomarenko took the salute alongside other Party luminaries. The final order to the partisans was to, 'start preparations for (their) disbandment'.